D0810574

HOOKED ON BOOKS

EVERYBODY'S GUIDE TO BOOK COLLECTING

by Maurice Dunbar

with special guest chapters by
Michael J. Quigley, M.D., Ph.D.
and Dennis M. Taugher

SMART'S PUBLISHING GROUP
San Mateo, California

ii

Hooked on Books is a new edition of *Books and Collectors* by Maurice Dunbar, originally published in 1980 by Book Nest, Los Altos, California.

Published by Smart's Publishing Group
One Waters Park Drive, Suite 104
San Mateo, California 94403

Jacket design by Rick Wong Design, San Francisco, California

Library of Congress Catalog Card Number: 97-065549

ISBN Number 0-9654129-4-6

Printed in the United States of America

10 9 8 7 6 5 4 3 2 1

Introduction to the Foreword

Warren Howell succeeded his father, John Howell, who founded the rare book dealership in San Francisco known internationally as "John Howell Books." Warren kindly wrote a foreword for my book, Books and Collectors, *which was published in 1980. Mr. Howell has since passed away and the 16 years intervening have rendered some of his foreword obsolete. Nevertheless, discriminating bibliophiles will remember him with pleasure and should appreciate what he had to say.*

FOREWORD

I WAS BROUGHT UP in a home filled with many books for both the reader and the collector. I became actively interested in collectors' books when I joined my father's rare book business in San Francisco in July of 1932. This was eight years after he had moved to 434 Post Street. Soon after entering this absorbing and fascinating business I realized that I must spend a great deal of time reading books about books, as I knew that I would never have the time to study the contents of all the books that we handled. Another must was to read the important books about book collecting. Books about books and collecting have been published continuously ever since Richard De Bury's *Philobiblion* was first printed in the 15th century.

The books that I first turned to and devoured were those by A. Edward Newton. I had heard my father speak many times of his friendship with Mr. Newton and particularly about his first visit to Mr. Newton's home at Daylesford, Penn. in 1918. It was at that time that Mr. Newton told him that his *Amenities of Book Collecting* was soon to be published in book form. My father said, "I'll buy a hundred copies of this book if you will inscribe them all." I know that my father sold these books quickly. I have read all of Mr. Newton's books, some of them two or three times, and I have tried to urge all of my customers to do the same. His anecdotes about the contents and the bibliographical points of books are fascinating to me. It has been said that more people were stimulated to take up book collecting by reading A. Edward Newton than any other author. Nearly all of the collectors' books mentioned with so much charm in Mr. Newton's books are still valuable books, and even more so today.

Mr. Dunbar's excellent book is written for the collector of modest means; that is, a collector who cannot aspire to collect on the scale of a J. Pierpont Morgan or a Henry E. Huntington. We have been instructing collectors, whenever possible, to learn the rules of the game in buying books, so that they may end up with a collection of which they can be justly proud. Mr. Dunbar demonstrates this beautifully in his book.

Naturally, he stresses the importance of the condition of the volumes. I will always remember my father saying, in talking about modern first editions, "We do not sell books; we sell condition."

I agree wholeheartedly with everything in this volume. If the collector does pay attention to everything in this book, he will avoid many mistakes made by the beginner.

This excellent guide is also a superb reference book, as it explains those mysterious symbols that denote the size and the format of the book. The chapters on "Latin Phrases," "Words and Abbreviations Commonly Found in English Language Publications," and the "System of Roman Numerals" are just some of the reasons the book should be kept at hand as a ready reference. The... [bibliography] is an excellent guide.

Warren Howell
San Francisco, Calif.
November 1979

PREFACE

FEW OF US CAN assemble collections such as those of Jerome Kern or William Andrews Clark. However, we can have a lifetime of learning and pleasure in book collecting with manageable expenditures of time and money. It is challenging, fun, exciting and often exasperating. It is somewhat introverted perhaps, yet strangely social. It is the current of life— dealing with people and books.

If you are just beginning to get serious about your own collecting, if you have observed the symptoms of bibliophilia in yourself, you may find some well-meant suggestions helpful. Or more commonly, if you have been considering emerging from being a mere accumulator to becoming an organized collector, your best move might be to read a book like this. Another good book to start with would be Charlie Lovett's *Everybody's Guide to Book Collecting*. Order postpaid $9.95 from: Write Brain Publishers, 10714 W 128th Ct., Suite 201, Overland Park, KS 66213.

There are many fine books available to inform, amuse, advise and direct the sophisticated collector (see bibliography for a representative list). There is a plethora of books about books, most of them well done by competent authors, but there are hardly any for the beginning amateur of limited resources. Those that claim to be for the neophyte almost always backslide into the esoteric, the erudite and the expensive. One excellent publication of this nature makes it no further than Page 17 until the author is blithely discussing a $3,600 book.

Now I have no proletarian contempt for the plutocracy. In fact, I think there should be a great many more rich folk. It is just that, as Lincoln observed, God must have loved poor people since he made so many of them. And poor people can have fun collecting books, too.

The present book is not designed for the affluent bibliomaniac. It is not intended for the learned curator of rare books with the funding of a rich alumni association. The book is not for the Rosenbachs and Weinsteins of the antiquarian book profession.

This book was written for the intellectually curious, the reader of books, the literate, the educated (formally or otherwise) amateur to whom the idea of book collecting is appealing. The book addresses not the indigent, not Jack London's "People of the Abyss" or those "Down and Out in Paris and London," but those who are working, making a living, paying their bills and buying books whenever they can. Both the plutocrat and the proletarian are necessarily excluded. If one is a baseball player or a talk-show host, he or she can simply buy a library or an antiquarian dealership of his own. If indigent, he can't afford good books or a place to keep them.

The present work is the result of hundreds of man-hours spent over the past 40 years in used bookstores, antiquarian book shops, second-hand stores, yard sales, garage sales, flea markets, libraries and private collections, both in the U.S. and abroad. In the course of my travels, I have, at last count (I keep a little journal), personally visited 109 university libraries.

Since 1981, I have been librarian for the San Jose, Calif. Scottish Rite (Masonic) Temple Library, which now has nearly 3,000 volumes of carefully selected first printings (mostly) in dust jackets of non-fiction books of special interest to the Lodge.

Having been, like François Villon, only a poor Master of Arts all these years, I have had to develop book-acquiring techniques without the luxury of ample funds or expense accounts. Merging a voracious appetite for books with a limited capacity for making money produces, if nothing else, resourcefulness. Book collecting takes abounding energy, the patience of a monk and the persistence of a mosquito.

Since we will be concerned primarily with books that working people (as opposed to the idle rich and the idle poor) can afford and can relate to, discussion of the rare and expensive will be curtailed. Thus the subject matter will be largely modern collectible books—not illuminated manuscripts, incunabula or grotesquely costly rare treasures.

In dealing with bibliographical examples, I have drawn heavily upon the Steinbeck canon. I have access to a friend's world-class collection at present and I once assembled a major collection of my own. I sold that collection in April 1984 and it is now intact in a library in Fukuoka, Japan.

I now have serious collections of Van Wyck Brooks, Barbara Tuchman, Stephen Birmingham, Joseph Wambaugh, Robert Ingersoll and Clarence Darrow. As Masonic librarian, I have collected works about George Washington (120 vol.), Benjamin Franklin, Andrew Jackson and Harry Truman. I have also assiduously hunted over much of the country for books on Freemasonry.

Anecdotes and stories have been disguised at times to avoid vulnerability but all events related have really occurred. Only the names and places have been changed or omitted.

ACKNOWLEDGEMENTS

IN 1980 I PUBLISHED *Books and Collectors*, which was mentioned kindly by Warren Howell in the "Foreword." In the 17 years since, the book was well treated by bookmen and I was encouraged in recent years to rewrite, expand, revise, correct and update it. But the person who really got behind it and provided material support was James Whitaker of Smart's Publishing Group—at the urging of bookman Dennis Taugher.

In November 1981 I joined the Scottish Rite of Freemasonry at the San Jose, Calif. Temple. I had originally joined the Masons in Topeka, Kan. in 1960 but had procrastinated going on to the advanced degrees. Immediately upon becoming a 32nd degree Mason, the secretary of the Temple appointed me orator and librarian. That secretary was Sam Nixon and I want to thank him and Leo Mark and all of the Venerable Masters since 1982 who had the confidence in me to appoint me each year to the responsible position of orator and librarian of the Scottish Rite Temple. It has indeed been an honor and a privilege.

In 1974 at Foothill College in Los Altos Hills, Calif., a few students and I started a little campus club of book collectors. We gave it a name as pompous as we could: The Foothill Bibliophile Society. Little could we know that 21 years later, that little club would expand to about 30 members and would be flourishing more than ever. I would be remiss and ungrateful if I did not mention with pleasure those members since 1974: Paul Martin (now of Bristol, Conn.), Elizabeth Olsen (now of Santa Barbara, Calif.), Chris Larsen, still active in the Society, and Anatol Lubovich, one of our earliest recruits. Dr. Ed and Mrs. Joan Sprague also have more than 20 years with us and Joan has been our secretary for many years.

Perhaps it is not appropriate under "Acknowledgments," but since I have digressed somewhat already, let me tell you something about the Society. We have no rules, no officers, no charter and no dues. To pay for postage for our newsletter, we assess members from time to time. We take turns acting as host for the group. It is the duty of the host to provide a meeting place (usually his or her home) and a guest speaker. When it is my turn, ordinarily in February, I have the group meet at the Scottish Rite Library. We meet the last Saturday evening each month except December, at which time we meet for a holiday buffet at the home of Ed and Anne-Marie Schmitz of Los Altos. Ed is the proprietor of the Book Nest Book Store. His store published my book, *Books and Collectors,* in 1980.

We bring books to meetings for "show and tell" or for sale. We all know each other's collecting habits so we often find choice books for other people in the club.

In December 1982, we went on a Caribbean cruise and at dinner the first evening, I met Michael J. Quigley, M.D., Ph.D., epidemiologist, editor, author, world traveler, career military physician, etc., etc. No "acknowledgment" could do justice to this man. Suffice it to say that he comes the closest to the Renaissance polymath of anyone I have met or heard of. Musician, mathematician, art and drama critic, but most significantly, one of the world's premier book collectors. I prevailed upon him to write a chapter for this new book. See the chapter "Book Collecting—The Hobby That Changed My Life."

CONTENTS

iii   FOREWORD

v   PREFACE

ix   ACKNOWLEDGEMENTS

1   WHAT IS A BOOK COLLECTOR

11   FIRST EDITIONS

21   OLD BOOKS

25   LIMITED EDITIONS

29   THE BEST SELLER PHENOMENON

35   LITERARY PRIZES

43   FOREIGN LANGUAGE EDITIONS

49   BOOK CLUB EDITIONS

53   AUTOGRAPHS AND INSCRIPTIONS

59   CARE, HANDLING AND CONDITION

77   MORE ON HANDLING BOOKS

81   BOOKS AS INVESTMENTS

87   LIBRARIES AND COLLECTORS

91   CONCERNING PUBLISHING COMPANIES

97   DEALING WITH THE DEALER

111   OTHER COLLECTIONS

117   MISCELLANEOUS SOURCES OF BOOKS

127   AN ESSAY ON BOOKS

131   LES NOMMES DE PLUME

139   PHOTOGRAPHY AND THE BOOK COLLECTOR

145   SOUND RECORDING

147   BOOK COLLECTING—THE HOBBY THAT CHANGED MY LIFE
       by Michael Quigley, M.D., Ph.D.

157   BOOK COLLECTING ON THE WEB
       by Dennis M. Taugher

167   SIZE OF BOOKS OR FORMAT

171   THE COLLECTOR IN CONCLUSION

175   GLOSSARY

189   ABBREVIATIONS

193   LATIN PHRASES, WORDS, AND ABBREVIATIONS COMMONLY
       FOUND IN ENGLISH LANGUAGE PUBLICATIONS

199   THE SYSTEM OF ROMAN NUMERALS

201   BOOKS ABOUT BOOKS

209   PERIODICALS

211   INDEX

WHAT IS A BOOK COLLECTOR?

WHAT DO THESE PEOPLE have in common:

Cicero	Wilhelm Rothschild
Henry I of England	Amy Lowel
Diane de Poitiers	William E. Gladstone
Cosimo di Medici	Eugene Field
Jules Cardinal Mazarin	Jean Hersholt
Samuel Pepys	Jerome Kern
Marie Antoinette	J. K. Lilly
George III	J. Pierpont Morgan
Henry E. Huntington	Louis Untermeyer

Among other possibilities, they were all book collectors. Are you a book collector? What exactly is a book collector? What is the difference between someone who possesses a lot of books and a collector?

Perhaps we can discuss the questions by analogy and example. I have several coins of various ages and values in my pockets, in my desk drawer, in the ashtray of my car. I often handle coins, yet I am not a coin collector. I often buy stamps and delight in the many different pictures and portraits on them. Yet I am not a stamp collector.

Merely possessing books, in however great numbers, does not make a collector. I remember a professor I had as a graduate student who offered to have our small seminar out to his house to see his book collection. I could not believe it. He had shelves built some eight feet high on both sides of a long hall in his big house. The shelves were beautifully built, adjustable and filled with the most dismally disappointing conglomeration of old text books, condensed books and book club editions that I had seen since the last thrift store I had visited. And this had been assembled by a Phi Beta Kappa Ph.D., a full professor. An accumulation is not a collection.

One might expect professional scholars, such as teachers, writers, editors and such to be collectors, but it is seldom the case. Wallace Stegner was always bemused but good-naturedly indulgent at us collectors of his work. He didn't even have first editions of most of his own nearly 30 titles. Most avid readers seem to have no regard for books as collectibles. They could not care less whether a book is a first printing or a third printing of the fourth edition or whether it is bound in paper or morocco. Their interest is only in the content.

The devoted reader and user of books is not necessarily, in fact, is not often a book collector. Having hundreds of books in one's home does not make a collection. Then what are we talking about?

A collection must have a theme—a guiding purpose, a goal— and must be motivated and organized with the theme or purpose in mind. Themes or subjects have characteristic features. Perhaps the most typical of all themes or the most popular is the author collection. Collect the author whose work you love. Collecting should be a labor of love. Certain authors have the magic gift of generating loyalty, devotion, affection and even a certain discipline in their readers. With those motives and some study and applied energy, anyone can have wonder and pleasure in "playing with your books." For example, the late Robert D. Fellman of Palo Alto, Calif. once made his home into a Dickensian library and museum. Dickens has the charm to engender that kind of adulation. Mr. Fellman donated his collection to Worcester Polytechnic Institute of Worcester, Mass. The Dickensian scholar, Dr. Joel Brattin, was instrumental in bringing the collection to W.P.I. The Fellman Collection may very well be the finest of its kind in the Western Hemisphere.

Another sort of collection is geographical. One of the members of our bibliophile society combines the "author" collection with the geographical, as her library is primarily concerned with books about Nebraska and works by a Nebraska author, Willa Cather. "City" collections are fun. There are enough books about San Francisco and famous or infamous San Franciscans to stock a silo. Books about London are wonderfully diverse and interesting.

Historical characters can be the subjects of fine collections. Lincoln, Napoleon, Franklin, Frank Lloyd Wright, Rommel, Darrow, MacArthur, Will Rogers, Babe Ruth and, of course, hundreds of others have been the focus of collecting effort. An interesting feature of this kind of collection is that nearly all of the books will be about the subject, not by the subject. One might make a collection of books, articles, essays, etc. about, say, Walt Whitman. It would be a challenge and a real work of scholarship even though the first printings of the work of Whitman himself would be virtually unobtainable. Nearly all of the first editions are in great institutional libraries such as the premier collection of Whitman at Duke University.

In Glen Ellen, Calif., in the heart of the beautiful wine country of the Napa Valley, there is a bookstore that is practically a monument to Jack London. It is not far from the old burned-out Wolf House of the author, nor is it far from his grave. The store has a "Jack London Room" and a unique collection of dozens of editions, issues and translations of a single title: *The Call of the Wild*. It is a magnificent example of the "One Book" or "Single Title" collection.

If you have a very special favorite book, perhaps *The Rubaiyat* or *The Spoon River Anthology*, you may want to own various editions of a single title. Ed and Anne-Marie Schmitz of Los Altos, Calif. have more than 140 different printings of *A Christmas Carol* This is by no means a mindless compilation of the same thing over and over. Each edition will have its own characteristics: Prefaces, introductions, biographical sketches, illustrations, book and type design, format, binding, date and place of publication—all will vary from edition to edition.

Sometimes a "single book" collection can be combined with another vocation or interest. A housewife of Buckley, Wash. is a serious Bible student and her collection consists of different translations of the Bible, all in English, everything from Wycliffe and Tyndale to *The New English Bible.*

Many books lend themselves well to a single-book collection. One is *The Divine Comedy.* Originally in 14th century Italian, it has been translated into English many times. My own favorite is that of John Ciardi.

Homer with his two great epics would keep a collector busy with various translations (all in English), from Chapman to T.E. Lawrence.

Chaucer's *Canterbury Tales,* Malory's *Le morte d'Arthur* and other classics produce "new and improved" translations from time to time. And if you read any foreign languages, your opportunities would be greatly expanded.

Probably the most logical collection would be one that was naturally compatible with one's profession. Although he is a patent attorney, a colleague collects biographies of inventors. He is an authority on the history of American technology. A mycologist has a library of books on mushrooms and toadstools. A dermatologist has assembled a collection about skin diseases from all over the world. A jeweler may hunt for books about gemstones and precious metals. I know a police officer who likes books written by law enforcement people. He has a very fine first edition of each of the 14 best sellers written by Joseph Wambaugh.

Although a collection compatible with one's work would seem to be almost expected, it is by no means universal. Some collectors prefer the exact opposite—an interest far different from their careers. A pharmacist collects books about opera. A chemistry teacher collects Dickens. A car salesman collects books about the Holocaust.

As you may agree, there are about as many subjects for book collecting as there are subjects. If any notion has flickered across the lower left-hand corner of a human mind, someone has written a book about it.

While literary subjects—poetry, fiction, drama, etc.—are wonderfully rich, literary work is but one area of interest and challenge for those who love books. With all of the permutations of possible subjects, the number of possible themes for the bibliophile is practically infinite. In a book printed in 1925 I read that it would take more than 500 years for a person to complete all of the courses then offered at Yale.

A resourceful postal inspector has a library of trivia—or as he prefers, significa. This is a venerable subject with ancestral works in the medieval books of hours, books of days, and the later almanacs. On his shelves are to be found books of lists, records, dates, books of maps, and esoterica of vast variety. He has specialized encyclopedias and dictionaries such as dictionaries of glass, of wine, of guns, food, trees, etc.

So there is frequently no particular connection between the collector's profession and his library. A. Edward Newton was an electronics manufacturer; J. Pierpont Morgan was a banker; Jerome Kern a composer and Adrian Goldstone was a textiles manufacturer.

Once Robert Frost was asked for a definition of poetry. The crusty old Yankee replied that poetry was what poets write. Thus a book collector is a person who makes a book collection. But, of course, that is too easy. We find that a precise definition of a collection is pretty elusive, but some progress can be made during a coherent discussion. We may agree that a collection requires a theme. It needs direction, arrangement and organization. Such basic elements would apply to most collections and are not, obviously, the sole property of book collecting.

A collection must be a challenge. As we saw in the story of my old professor, all he had to do was join the book club, pay his bills and shelve each selection as it arrived in the mail. That's no fun. If gold were as common as feldspar, who would covet it? The collection must have some worth, some value, some gravity. Or at least, the collector must think so. The subject of the collection must be in demand, or it must have potential demand. For example, a new copy of a first edition of a current best seller may have little value now (the publisher's price) but may be worth many times that price twenty years from now. In order to be a worthwhile collection, I think it must evoke a little envy from other book lovers. Friendly and generous envy, of course, but a little envy nevertheless. Who envies the possessor of a wall full of *Readers' Digest* condensed books? Maybe for insulation, but not as collectors' items. You may enjoy keeping your old textbooks, but don't call it a collection. One consolation about such books: They are not apt to be stolen.

A collection must have some value. It must generate some pride of ownership. If you have a garage full of book club editions, broken sets, etc. and this makes you happy, peace, brother. But don't call yourself a book collector. If you have a lot of books in ragged condition, without dust jackets or highlighted with hideous yellow marking ink and you enjoy them, that's your business. But don't expect anyone else to want them, even if they're free.

It is human nature for one to enjoy being admired or respected for his judgment. This applies to the world of bibliophilia as intensely as to the business or professional world. Your collection will never be admired or respected if there is no demand or esteem for it.

Demand without scarcity, however, merely produces a best seller. If the first printing of a book was 100,000 copies, it is unlikely that it will ever have much collectible value. It is too common, too easily obtained. Scarcity, on the other hand, is worthless without demand.

This is not to say that in order to be of value a book must fetch high prices in the world book market. A collection may have integrity, coherence and be useful and gratifying to its owner without having great monetary value. This may appear contradictory to the previous paragraph, but it is true. Many superlative works of scholarship have simply never caught on as collector's items. None of the books of Van Wyck Brooks are especially expensive. Yet Brooks was one of the best of literary historians, critics and biographers. He was a fine writer—accurate, erudite, witty and humorous. His *The Flowering of New England* (NY: E.P. Dutton, 1936) won a Pulitzer Prize for non-fiction and was issued in slipcase for the Limited Editions Club in 1941. The LEC is listed in a 1992 catalog for $65. Literary history and biography are seldom in the same league of pricing as fiction and poetry by famous authors. Hence Brooks' books, in spite of their superior quality, have only a lukewarm demand in the market.

A first edition of the children's story *The Wizard of Oz* by L. Frank Baum would no doubt fetch more money than all of the brilliant scholarship of Van Wyck Brooks combined (more than 20 titles over a period of more than 40 years). However, don't expect much of anything in the world of collecting to make sense. After all, Danielle Steel has sold more books than Hemingway and Faulkner combined.

Each book collection is unique. Each has had impinged upon it the personality of a unique person. Each of us has a different sense of importance, emphasis, arrangement and interest. Each person becomes a collector in his own way. Probably no one ever made a New Year's resolution to become a book collector. Few people, I suspect, have ever been persuaded into the hobby by someone else. It does not lend itself to Eric Hoffer's "holy cause" or "mass movement" phenomenon. In all probability, most collectors have taken up their particular theme by sheer fortuitous coincidence. In talking with dozens of collectors over many years, I have often inquired as to what induced them to begin their collections. Usually it is a story of some event, often casual, that occurred to divert their interest into a particular area. Frequently, a great collection begins with the acquiring of a single book, perhaps a gift. "A journey of a thousand miles begins with one step," said Confucius.

During the Vietnam War, an American college student was "vacationing" in Canada and was detained as a draft dodger. He was made a guest of the Canadian authorities and while partaking of their hospitality, found a book in the room they had provided for him. It was Martha Rofheart's *Fortune Made His Sword*. It was such a wonderful biographical novel based on the life and times of Henry V that the student eventually became a teacher of history himself. It was the initial spark—a cheap, well-worn paperback—that led to serious scholarship and collecting.

During the one year that I taught high school I was assigned a sophomore English class. The class consisted mostly of students returning from "continuation school," an arrangement which attempts to educate juvenile disciplinary cases who really don't want to be in school at all. They are rarely any better after returning to the regular classroom.

After trying every resource at my disposal without much success, I went to the vice principal. He told me that if no one was hurt during the class to consider it a good day. Well, that was no help, so at lunch (I lived across the street) I discussed the situation with my wife. She advised that I try reading to them. What would it hurt?

I had recently bought a copy of Steinbeck's *Of Mice and Men*. I had just started reading Steinbeck's works and this was one I had not yet read. So I might accomplish something even if the students didn't.

Thus I began to read *Of Mice and Men* to that room full of apprentice criminals, wannabe hoods and sullen, unhappy girls. Soon, much to my delight, I had their attention. If anyone made a sound, someone else would tell him to shut up and listen. When the bell rang, they groaned with resentment that they had to leave. In the following days, several of them came to class sick or injured so they wouldn't miss the continuing story of Lennie and George. On the day we finished the book, one of the worst trouble-makers came up to me after the class had left and asked, "Did that guy Steinbeck write any other books?" That was the day that I resolved to own a first edition of everything Steinbeck ever wrote. Of course, I never acquired everything, but by 1984 when I sold the collection, it consisted of more than 600 items.

To many people, a "favorite son" author is appealing. A Hoosier may collect Dreiser or a Nebraskan may collect Cather (even if she was born in Virginia). The Scottish Rite Masonic Temple of McAlester, Ok. collects everything by or about Will Rogers. Almost routinely, state universities collect material about their states, people, history, geology, etc. A bibliophile of Palatka, Fla. has a "favorite daughter" collection of Marjorie Kinnan Rawlings.

The subject or theme collection, besides its intrinsic interest, has a tremendous advantage over other varieties of book collecting. The range of subject matter is virtually infinite. The subject collection permits a maximum latitude of expression of the collector's personality, his idiosyncrasies and special knowledge. The subject collection works well with and often derives from another hobby. Incidentally, I don't like the fatuous word "hobby," which has connotations of a frivolous or "made work" use of time—something to keep the inmates busy. However, we do not have a suitable word in English for the skilled and devoted work of the dedicated amateur. In many cases, one's "hobby" turns out to be his significant life's work and his profession merely a means of supporting the hobby. A book collecting hobby, particularly of the "subject" type, is often a "spin off" from something else.

An army officer, now deceased, learned to use rifles, rim-fire and center-fire; open, peep and 'scope sighted; target and sporting, all before he was out of grammar school. By the time he was in college, he was widely known as a marksman. After ROTC, he spent 20 years in the infantry and military police, where his knowledge and skill served him well. Over the years, he collected books about firearms, their history and their technology. In time he had an impressive collection, highly specialized, well organized and well cared for. He had at no time intended to become a book collector, per se. He had just graduated into the hobby as a useful part of the military career he had chosen.

Incidentally, the many fine collections of the public libraries and the universities are nearly always bequeathed to them by individual collectors. The White (White Motor Co.) Collection of orientalia is a good example. The White also has what is perhaps the best collection of chess books in existence. Cleveland, Oh. is justly proud of their great public library.

The Philadelphia Free Library has one of the best collection of Dickens in the Western Hemisphere. Boston, Detroit, New York, Chicago and Oakland are a few more public libraries with fine special collections. And I have already mentioned the Fellman Collection in Worcester, Mass.

I have personally visited 109 university libraries, including the University of Beijing and Lomonosov University in Moscow, and all of them are the beneficiaries of the generosity of private collectors.

Most of the wonderful collections remind us that books, like wine and oxygen, mix well with almost anything else.

We see that sometimes an attempt to define something like book collecting consists of describing what it is not and in citing examples. A collection may be analogous to a Rorschach Test: One brings to it the knowledge, wisdom, lore, learning and sensibilities of a lifetime.

In all probability, since you are reading a book about book collecting, you have already begun to collect. So I need not convince you of the glories, pleasures and profits of the world's premier hobby. It is a pretty safe guess that you are already with us.

First Editions

The prices paid for first editions are no real evidence of the value of a book or the eminence of an author. Indeed, the "first edition" hobby is one of the minor forms of mental derangement, seldom ending in homicide, and outside the scope of the law.

—Stephen Leacock

IN A LECTURE ON book collecting, the speaker passed among the group two books. One was a custom-bound, blind stamped maroon calf volume with all edges gold, a printing of the works of Samuel Coleridge (1772 - 1834). It was an illustrated edition on fine paper, dated 1879 and in pristine condition. The other book was a cheaply cased third-rate novel in a repaired dust jacket of a gaudy, juvenile design. It had been a publishing failure and had been remaindered.

The exercise was to decide which book was the more valuable. The cheap novel ($2.50 in 1929) was Steinbeck's first book, *Cup of Gold*[1] and it was worth about $3,000 in 1995. The beautiful gold and leather volume of first-rate English poetry (more than a hundred years old) was worth perhaps $20.

---

[1]Robert M. McBride of New York printed 2,476 copies, of which 939 were remaindered to Max Salop of the Harlem Book Co. These unbound sheets were later bound and issued by Covici-Friede Co., constituting the second edition of *Cup of Gold*.

The reason for the great difference in value may be explained in one word: demand. For the past 50 years, Steinbeck has been collected but in the past 20 years, collectors have multiplied and their enthusiasm intensified. And those factors have been magnified by the general inflation of all prices. The Steinbeck collection that I sold in 1984 for $24,500 (the broker told me $24,000 and charged me a 25 percent commission besides) would easily be worth $50,000 today. *Cup of Gold* was Steinbeck's first book (a good reason in itself to collect the book) and is extremely scarce.

On the other hand, the shelves of the antiquarian bookstores are usually loaded with attractive reprints of 19th century English poets and there is little demand for them. The Coleridge book described in this anecdote would probably sell as a decorator's item.

It is not enough, in order to be an economist, to repeat the simplistic phrase "supply and demand." Many subtleties and variables apply to this challenging, if dismal, science. However, the book trade conforms remarkably closely to this economic cliché.

Both factors must exist. There must be a demand and a scarcity. If there is a demand, however powerful, and an abundant supply, the result is merely a best seller. If there is a scarcity and no demand, the article will have no value. Even if there is only one copy in the world, if no one wants it, it is worthless. A book, like anything else, is worth only what someone is willing to pay for it.

Incidentally, the prices for new books here in the mid-1990s are great bargains—if the relative purchasing power of former times is compared to the present. Remember that *Cup of Gold* was priced at $2.50 in 1929 and prices remained pretty much the same throughout the 1930s. A comparable book today would retail for about $20. During the '30s, one could hire a construction or farm laborer to work 10 hours for $2.50. Today that laborer would make about $60 for an eight-hour day.

The public is often exposed to the term "first edition." A student once left me a note: "My father has some first additions that he wants you to look at." A typical ad might have "includes some first editions." Many bookstores have special sections labeled "First Editions." So what is so significant about first editions of books?

One element of collectibility of first editions is that of scarcity. Publishers usually (unless the author is already a best-selling writer) rather gingerly produce first editions in moderate numbers. If the book doesn't sell, then the publisher doesn't have many copies to "eat" or dispose of. Disposal normally consists of selling the remaining copies to a book merchant called a "remainder house." This is usually a certain loss. If the book sells well and demand is sustained, new printings can always be ordered. Thus many coveted titles have a history of having been printed in small numbers in the first edition. Michener's first book, *Tales of the South Pacific*, published when he was a 40-year-old Navy veteran with no publishing track record to speak of, is now very rare in the first printing. As a Pulitzer Prize winner and the basis for a Broadway musical, subsequent editions were produced in large numbers. The early works of most authors exhibit this phenomenon.

Another appeal of first editions is a subtle one. Just as the antique collector rejects reproductions with scorn, the book collector shuns reprints. The collector of paintings is not content with prints or facsimiles. The attitude of the bibliophile is quite the same. He wants the original, the first. It is this factor that is the least rational to the normal person, i.e., the non-collector. Why someone will pay $1,000 or more for a first edition when a $10 reprint will read just as well confounds and perplexes the mind of the average citizen.

Furthermore, with books there is the matter of scholarship. The bibliophile collects the wisdom, the ideas and the memory of the human race. He wants the material in as pristine condition as possible. He wants to see the original work free of revision, editing, condensation or modification. First editions are usually the only editions personally supervised by the author. Unless he does a revised or enlarged edition, the first printing will ordinarily be the only one with which he was personally concerned.

It is a reliable rule that the first edition of a book will be the most valuable issue. However, in the world of books, generalizations are more than normally risky. Just as you have learned some good axioms, exceptions appear.

For example, the first edition of Edward F. Ricketts' *Between Pacific Tides* (Stanford University Press, 1938) is less in demand than the second edition (1948), which contains the introduction by Steinbeck.

Limited Editions Club (LEC) books are often worth more than the first editions of the same titles. A first of Van Wyck Brooks' Pulitzer

Prize (non-fiction) book, *The Flowering of New England* (NY: Dutton, 1937) is worth about $25. The LEC of 1938, fine in slipcase, should bring $75.

Collector demand is the key factor in the value of any collectible item. In first editions, it makes all the difference. It must be maddening to Steinbeck's critics to observe how his books have increased in value almost exponentially since his death. A fine first edition of *The Grapes of Wrath* was $60 in 1975. (I bought it at John Howell Books in San Francisco.) A fine first of that old Pulitzer Prize novel is now $1,000. There were 19,806 copies in the first printing—hardly a rare book.

In the LEC *Grapes of Wrath* edition, there were 1,146 copies. It was uniquely bound in wheat straw and rawhide, issued in slipcase in two volumes and illustrated and signed by the great painter, Thomas Hart Benton. It should be worth more than the first edition (i.e., the Viking Press trade edition), but it is not. A plain case of intense collector demand for the first edition. Steinbeck, like Lancelot, goes galloping down the generations, gathering readers' hearts on his lance like tilting rings.

First editions are not the only editions that have collectibility. Besides the elegant limited reprints, ordinary second and third editions of *Cup of Gold, To a God Unknown,* and *The Pastures of Heaven* (just to mention three) have substantial value.[2]

Many elements can produce variation in the value of books besides its being a first edition. If a reprint copy or a book club edition has an interesting provenance, autographs or inscriptions, it can well be worth more than an ordinary first edition.

As an author's reputation develops, his publisher will ordinarily produce larger numbers of his books in the first printings. The supply increases and the scarcity therefore diminishes. Books published late in the career of a popular author are usually inexpensive. Allen and Patricia Ahearn's fine *Collected Books, the Guide to Values* (1991) indicates that William Faulkner's first book *The Marble Faun* (1924) is worth $20,000. *Intruder in the Dust*, published when the author was at the height of his popularity in 1948, is worth a mere $200.

This is an appropriate place to point out something about bibliophilia that is not particularly obvious. One must keep in mind that the worth of a publication as a work of art, as a contribution

---

[2] Remember that I am only considering copies in fine condition in the original.

to the civilization of mankind, very often has nothing to do with its value as a collector's item. *The Marble Faun* is a small book of indifferent poetry while *Intruder* is a fine novel by a Nobel Prize author at the prime of his genius.

But the 1924 book is the author's first book and nearly all of them were inscribed to friends. Since they wouldn't sell, Faulkner made presents of most of them. To see the finest collection of Faulkner, by the way, one needs to go to the University of Virginia at Charlottesville. While there, you can see the holograph manuscript of *The Grapes of Wrath*.

The beginner would be well advised to collect a contemporary author or even more than one author. That would enable the collector to acquire the early works of the writer at reasonable cost. Examples of outstanding contemporary authors with established reputations and promising futures: James D. Houston, Dean Ing, John Irving, Larry McMurtry, Stephen King, Barbara Kingsolver, Louise Erdich, Elizabeth Tallent. An absurdly minute list; there are hundreds.

First edition mania does not apply to reference books, textbooks, dictionaries or encyclopedias nearly as forcefully as to fiction. While the first editions of Johnson's (1755) or Webster's (1828) dictionaries are quite valuable,[3] generally speaking, reference books and textbooks become obsolete and practically valueless. A first edition of a high school algebra text dated 1936 would probably be hard to give away. With the exception of the eleventh edition of the *Encyclopedia Britannica*, most obsolete references have little more than curiosity value, unless, of course, they are very old, written by a famous author or have some interesting provenance. Exceptions abound.

IDENTIFYING FIRST EDITIONS

Now let us cautiously enter the great dismal swamp of first edition identity and definition. It is a formidable and complex subject.

In the United States, as well as in many other countries, the publishing business is a free enterprise. It is based upon profit

---

[3]For some indication of the world of dictionary collecting, see: *A Short-Title Catalogue of the Warren N. & Suzanne B. Cordell Collection of Dictionaries* (Terre Haute: Cunningham Memorial Library, Indiana State University, 1975), 212 pp.

and loss and operates under the impetus of competition like any other business. Publishing companies employ their individualism and each has its own style, customs, traditions and idiosyncrasies. Hence there is no uniformity in the practices of these companies in identifying their first editions. In some cases, it is simply not possible to determine the edition status of a book without a bibliography or special reference that deals with "points" identification. Those characteristics and features that constitute the points often require the most rigorous and meticulous scholarship to differentiate.

Older references such as Boutell's *First Editions of Today* and Merle Johnson's *American First Editions* (and their revisions) are very useful to collectors and dealers.

There are catalogs and bibliographies in existence about major authors and collectors' subjects. For example, if you collect Steinbeck, Adrian Goldstone and John Payne published a fine bibliography in 1974 which is accurate and comprehensive. Since Steinbeck died in 1968, the bibliography is virtually complete except for the posthumous material. Even so, perfection is impossible and many catalogs advertise collectors' items "not in Goldstone."

Most serious collectors have more than one collection and in addition to their regular collections, they collect bibliographies, catalogs and books about books.

The terminology employed in the book world is ambiguous, confusing, overlapping, inadequate and redundant in indicating the sequence in which books have been published. Nearly 70 years ago, H.S. Boutell was having the same problem:

> ...the correct term is not First Edition but First Impression or Issue. Unfortunately this error of terminology is almost universal; and it was felt that to use any but the usual phrase...would be to invite misapprehension. One hopes that a better state of things will one day prevail.[4]

Well, of course, a better state of things does not prevail. Indeed, the increasing number of publishers and publications in the past 70 years has exacerbated the situation.

---

[4]H.S. Boutell, *First Editions of Today* (Phila.: Lippincott, 1928). Publisher's note.

In compiling his book, Boutell had written to publishers asking them for information about identifying the first editions of their books. One of them, J.W. Arrowsmith of London, submitted the following:

> Our custom is to put on the back of the title page "First Published in 1928," or whatever the year may be. Reprints are marked "First published in 1928—second impression 1928" and so on.
>
> May we take this opportunity of pointing out that the words "First Edition" are invariably misused. What is meant is "First Impression" as a First Edition may include 20 or 30 impressions and presumably it is only the first of which is of value. (Boutell, p. 12)

In the United States, the term "printing" as in "first printing" is used. In Britain, the term "impression" is employed. The words are synonymous and interchangeable.

The first edition then is the first form in which a book appears. The content, format, type, pagination and design of all copies in the first edition are essentially the same. The publisher may put out, say, 5,000 copies—the number he estimates will sell. If the first impression (printing) sells out, he may produce another 5,000 (or any number) identical to the first batch. He may, in fact, repeat the process over and over, sometimes over a period of many years. For instance, Leonard Bloomfield's *Language* was published in 1933 and was reprinted unchanged for decades. As long as the book is unchanged it remains the first edition, even if it is not the first printing. The publisher may add such things as "65th thousand" or "7th big printing"—sort of boasting as it were. However, if the book is essentially the same, it is still the first edition.

So much for the "first edition" and "first printing." What about the term "first state"? Let us discuss a specific example. In the first state of the first printing of the first edition of *Of Mice and Men* (NY: Covici-Friede, 1937) p. 9, lines 20-21 read: "and only moved because the heavy hands were pendula." Steinbeck was unhappy with that particular diction and insisted that the lines be changed to: "His arms did not swing at his sides, but hung loosely." The copies with "hung loosely" are the second state. It was not a new printing but a minor change of the same printing of the first edition. Those lines are the only difference in the two states. Every

other feature of the two books is identical. Both are first editions.
Both are first printings. But they are not both the first state. The
first state, because it is the first and, incidentally, much more rare,
is the "First Edition" that all knowledgeable collectors want.
Ahearn (op.cit. p. 529) indicates that the first state is worth $450;
the second state $150. There is an even more trivial "point" in *Of
Mice and Men*. Page 88 has a dot or "bullet" between the 8s in the
first state; it is removed in the second state. So the second state is a
more nearly perfect book, but the first state is worth at least three
times as much. Such a minor change is a typical "point" in "first
edition" identification.

Then there is the subject of variants. Suppose that the binder
has contracted to bind 10,000 copies of a book, using green cloth.
After he has bound 8,472 copies, he runs out of green cloth.
Rather than default on his contract or delay the binding, he merely switches to some blue cloth that he has on hand. So all 10,000
copies of this first printing are absolutely identical except that the
first 8,472 are green and the remaining 1,528 are blue. Both the
green and the blue books are first printings of the first edition, but
obviously, they are not exactly alike. They are said to be variants.
In all probability, no one will remember or record which was
bound first and in future years, collectors will have to have both
variants to be sure that they have the first. An example of this
phenomenon is Steinbeck's book *The Log from the Sea of Cortez*.
There is one variant in aqua cloth and another in maroon. No
proof exists as to which is the first.

There are other forms of variants. The staining of the top edges
for one. Some tops may be green, some yellow, blue, etc. There
are variants of dust jackets. In the American edition of *1984* by
George Orwell, there is a red jacket and a blue jacket—both clearly indicating "First American Edition" on the copyright page.
Opinions of Oliver Allston by Van Wyck Brooks (NY: Dutton, 1941)
was published with some copies in turquoise dust jackets and
some in red. Both variants state "First Edition." The binding of
both is identical—light blue cloth.

Publishers, printers and binders rarely take any notice of such
trivia. Only bibliophiles concern themselves with such minutiae.
Hence publishers will usually have no idea which variant is first

and the primacy in variants may never be established. So the only safe course for the meticulous collector is to possess all variants.

It becomes apparent that when book collectors say "first edition," what they really mean is the first variant (if known) of the first state of the first printing of the first edition. And that is exactly what I mean in this book whenever the term "first edition" is used. The confusing situation is somewhat analogous to that of the English spelling system. We all know it to be an irrational anachronism but we are stuck with it.

As Van Allen Bradley has pointed out:

> *Very, very roughly speaking, this (first edition) means the first appearance of the work in question, independently, between its own covers. But, like many other household words, this apparently simple term is not always as simple as it appears. The question "When is a first edition not a first edition?" is a favourite debating exercise among bibliophiles and advanced collectors.*[5]

A first edition, as defined, is not a first edition when it is not a first variant of the first state of the first printing of the first edition. Nor when it is a pirated book. I have a copy of Joseph Wambaugh's *The Onion Field* (NY: Delacourt Press, 1973). On the copyright page of this copy, it states "First Printing, 1973." However, this book was photoprinted in Taiwan without regard to copyright. A pirated book, its dimensions don't even resemble the first edition.

Just because it plainly states "First Printing" or "First Edition" on the copyright page does not guarantee that the book is indeed a first. Many copies of William Faulkner's *The Reivers* state FIRST PRINTING but they are book club editions, as indicated by the blind stamping in the lower right hand corner of the back cover of the binding. Thus there are many instances when a first edition (so stated) is not a first edition. To properly identify the issue of your books you should have a special reference book designed for that purpose.[6]

---

[5]Van Allen Bradley, *More Gold in Your Attic* (NY: Fleet Pub. Co., 1961).

[6]See Zemple, *The Identification of First Editions.*

OLD BOOKS

A good book, in the language of book-sellers, is a saleable one; in that of the curious, a scarce one; in that of men of sense, a useful and instructive one.

— Chambers

IN THE LANGUAGE of many people, a good book is an old one. Every dealer in the world has had the experience of having someone bring books to him that are "old" (and therefore valuable) in the expectation of walking away counting their money. The "old" books usually date from the late 1800s or early 1900s.

Unless books are really old (medieval manuscripts or incunabula), age doesn't have much to do with the value of a book. My fine old eleventh edition of Robertson's *History of Scotland* is dated 1787 but probably would not bring over $30, whereas Larry McMurtry's *Lonesome Dove* was published in 1985 and Ahearn shows it to be worth $175. There are other factors so much more potent than mere age that the date of publication is relatively unimportant. Van Allen Bradley confirms this:

> *One of the commonest misconceptions about book collecting is that a book must be a couple of hundred years old to have attained any great value. Actually, many of the older books have very little commercial worth, simply because they are of no importance or are in plentiful supply. On the other hand, many modern books of*

*importance have become scarce and expensive because of
the demand for them.[7]*

The term "old" in describing books is such a vague and relative
word that it is not of much use. Even among distinguished collectors and booksellers there is considerable difference of opinion in
dealing with the question, "When is a book old?" One dealer stated that he would probably be interested in a book's age if printed
before 1800. Another replied that he would not be impressed with
the age of a book, per se, unless it were from the 17th century or
earlier.

Many other factors apply. The sheer importance of a book in the
intellectual history of humanity is a powerful element. A first edition of Huxley's *Brave New World*, published in 1932 (a relatively
recent book), would be much more valuable than some reprint of
a book of obscure homiletics printed in 1700. A copy of Sir
Edward Coke's *Commentaries* of 1628 is not valuable because it is
more than 300 years old. It is valuable because it is of importance
in the evolution of English law.

We should distinguish between "early" and "old." An early work
of Mark Twain (1835-1910) would have been published in the
1870s. A late work would be *A Double-Barreled Detective Story* (1902).
So his "early" work is not very old. A "late" work of François
Rabelais (1494-1553) would be old.

Age is such a relative feature. At 26, John Keats' life was over.
At 80, W.E.B. DuBois began a new career. At 15, homo sapiens is
an adolescent. At 15, a cat may be the patriarch of 14 generations.
So a hundred-year-old book is merely well established.

Condition is one of the most all-pervading and potent elements
in the entire universe of book collecting. As you might expect, this
feature accumulates gravity with the age of the item in question—
becoming more precious with the passage of time. Many "old"
books that people bring in to dealers for appraisal or sale are in
such an advanced state of decomposition that they may be reject-
ed out of hand. Unless printed by Gutenberg or Caxton, they are
rarely worth more than kindling.

---

[7]Van Allen Bradley, *More Gold in Your Attic* (NY: Fleet Pub. Co., 1961). Note
the operative word "demand."

Thus, we can conclude with a reasonable degree of confidence that age, per se, is not particularly indicative of either interest or value in a book. An "old" book must have essentially the same qualities as a recent one. It must be important (to someone), relatively scarce, in good condition and in demand.

Limited Editions

And the printer knew that the limited edition was not a racket as long as he had honesty and sincerity, and reverence for the best traditions of his craft.
— Edwin Grabhorn

THE FINEST BOOKS are a harmony of the best paper, the best ink, the most skilled hand-set type appropriately chosen or designed, and printed by a master craftsman with a hand press. In the tradition from Gutenberg to William Morris, all such fine books have been limited editions. That is, they were produced in small numbers. The cost of a Kelmscott Chaucer or a Grabhorn *Leaves of Grass* was such that if all books were so produced, we would be back to the Middle Ages when only the rich could afford books.

Fine press books are to mass-produced books as Rolls-Royces are to Fords. And how many of us would be automobile owners if it were not for Henry Ford and mass production? Of course, we lovers of books glow with admiration for the masterpieces of the book maker's art. We visit the shrines and temples where these treasures are kept, hat in hand. However, we ordinary middle class collectors cannot participate. We cannot entertain reasonable hopes of owning such books. We cannot even borrow such books.

Thus in discussing "limited editions," the discourse will be confined to those limited editions which are not fine press books. The limited editions at our not-so-rarefied altitude of bibliophilia will be those of the major publishers and Everyman and Everywoman will have a chance to own a few of them.

The limited editions of the regular publishers are normally not so outrageously priced as to be prohibitive to the average collector. The trade edition of Steinbeck's *Life in Letters* was $15 in 1975. A few months later, the limited edition was $35.

Most of the limited editions will be of better quality than the ordinary "trade" editions. Many are published in slipcases. They are usually numbered and many of them are signed, either by the author or the illustrator or both. The LEC *Grapes of Wrath* (1940) was signed by the illustrator, Thomas Hart Benton, but not by the author. The LEC *The Martian Chronicles* was signed by the author, Ray Bradbury, and by the illustrator, Joseph Mugnaini.

The most salient feature of a limited edition is that it be limited in numbers. Probably 2,500 copies would be the maximum number, so declared prior to publication, that could properly be called limited. Most such editions consist of far fewer than that. There were only 99 copies of the limited *In Dubious Battle* (1936) and the limited *The Red Pony* was 699. Occasionally, some of the copies of a limited edition are reserved and often those copies are not numbered. The limited *East of Eden* states: "This autographed first edition of *East of Eden* is limited to 1,500 copies, of which 750 are for private distribution." Naturally, those reserved copies are the most prized collector's items.

Slipcases, illustrations, superior paper and binding, autographs, etc. are all very nice, but none of these features makes a limited edition in and of themselves. The essence of the limited edition is the artificially induced scarcity. And there are several permutations upon that factor. The *East of Eden* example is only one of many.

Common sense would lead one to assume that the limited edition would be produced first, followed by the trade edition. This is the usual procedure in publishers' limited editions. Sometimes, however, the trade edition will be on the market for some time before the limited edition appears. This is opposed to the Limited Editions Club, whose publications are, by definition, reprints.

However, the scarcity, quality and frequently the superlative illustrations drive the prices of used LEC editions up. Since only subscribers of the LEC can obtain the books new, a collector who is not a member must wait until a member is willing to part with a book before the collector can acquire it. Some LEC titles are worth more than the publisher's first editions. This is particularly true with books that have been illustrated and signed by famous artists.

It must be made clear that this escalation of value of some of the LEC titles does not apply to all of them. Intensely collected authors and illustrators whose works appear in the LEC publications will be in great demand. Demand, combined with the deliberately limited numbers which produces the element of scarcity, produces elevated prices.

Some limited editions are the only editions. The Books Arts Club of the University of California produced some excellent books about books in limited numbers. *Byways in Bookland* by James Westfall Thompson was published in 1935 in 600 copies for club distribution. *About Books, a Gathering of Essays* was published in 1941 in 450 copies. No other editions of either book were ever made. Such publishing practice is quite common with books of limited or specialized appeal. One more example: Deborah Benson Covington (daughter of the great bibliophile, Ben Abramson) published *The Argus Book Shop: A Memoir* (W. Cornwall, Conn., Tarrydiddle Press, 1977). This wonderful little book is fascinating to bibliophiles who knew of her father and his bookstore in Chicago. Only 350 copies were printed and the plates were destroyed.

Many limited editions will have preview or subscription material loosely inserted in the volume. This may take the form of a card or brochure which described the book in advance of its publication. For example, when the Book Club of California issued *Valenti Angelo: Author, Illustrator, Printer,* each of the 950 members received a prospectus describing the forthcoming book. In most cases those who ordered and received a copy have inserted the brochure in the back of the book. This kind of material should never be discarded since it is practically impossible to replace, and although the book itself will not mention that ephemeral material exists, knowledgeable collectors expect to find it, since it adds to the interest and value of the book.

Some limited editions are essentially the same as the trade edition except that they are numbered, put in a cheap slipcase and sold for a premium price. Other "limited editions" are not limited at all. They are merely called limited editions. Typical of these would be the subscription type of marketing plan such as the Franklin Library operation. The customer usually agrees to buy all of the books in a given series, typically one each month. The offering is nationally advertised and no limitation upon "membership" is made. Erskine Caldwell was paid $50,000 for signing 25,000 copies of one of his titles. Hardly a limited edition. Although the Franklin Library and Easton Press (a similar book marketing operation) books are beautifully made, it is probably not what Ed Grabhorn had in mind.

THE BEST SELLER PHENOMENON

The Preacher sought to find out acceptable words...even words of truth...
And further by these, my son, be admonished; of making many books, there is no end.

— Koheleth

FROM ONE EXTREME to the other, we flip from limited editions to best sellers. The former limits production deliberately; the latter produces as many copies as it is possible to sell. The term "best seller" varies with time and geography. *Concerning Two Lovers* by Aeneas Sylvius (later Pope Pius II) was a best seller in the 15th century. However, in the time of the incunabula, a very modest number of copies (by modern standards) would constitute a best seller. Also, a best seller in Albanian or Basque would hardly compare with best sellers in English or French. The "best seller" in our context refers to a universal phenomenon regardless of the original language in which it was composed. Some of the best selling books become such only when translated. *Quo Vadis* was originally written in Polish and did not become a big seller until translated into the great imperial languages of English, French and Spanish. *All Quiet on the Western Front* (*Im Westen Nichts Neues*) sold more copies in English than in the original German.

Because of the vastly improved mass-production technology, rapid transportation and distribution combined with the greatly increased literacy and demand for books, nearly all of the best sellers of all time have been 20th century books.

Since this book is primarily concerned with fiction, the best selling cook books, baby care books, religious books and dictators' little red books will not be considered.

It does not seem to be true that becoming a best seller automatically disqualifies a work from the ranks of fine literature. Discriminating English teachers and critics alike can find some excellent books among the annual best sellers. The original language, if not English, is indicated.

THE BESTSELLERS IN FICTION SINCE 1895

1895 *Beside the Bonnie Brier Bush*, Ian Maclaren
1896 *Tom Grogan*, F. Hopkinson Smith
1897 *Quo Vadis* (Polish), Henry Sienkiewicz
1898 *Caleb West*, F. Hopkinson Smith
1899 *David Harum*, Edward N. Westcott
1900 *To Have and to Hold*, Mary Johnston
1901 *The Crisis*, Winston Churchill[8]
1902 *The Virginian*, Owen Wister
1903 *Lady Rose's Daughter*, Mrs. Humphrey Ward
1904 *The Crossing*, Winston Churchill
1905 *The Marriage of William Ashe*, Mrs. Humphrey Ward
1906 *Coniston*, Winston Churchill
1907 *The Lady of the Decoration*, Frances Little
1908 *Mr. Crewe's Career*, Winston Churchill
1909 *The Inner Shrine*, Anon. (Basil King)
1910 *The Rosary*, Florence Barclay
1911 *The Broad Highway*, Jeffrey Farnol
1912 *The Harvester*, Gene Stratton-Porter
1913 *The Inside of the Cup*, Winston Churchill
1914 *The Eyes of the World*, Harold Bell Wright
1915 *The Turmoil*, Booth Tarkington
1916 *Seventeen*, Booth Tarkington
1917 *Mr. Britling Sees It Through*, H.G. Wells

---

[8]The American novelist, Winston Churchill, is distinguished from the British prime minister by the latter's having a middle initial: Winston S. Churchill (1874-1964).

1918 *The U.P. Trail*, Zane Grey
1919 *The Four Horsemen of the Apocalypse* (Spanish), V. Blasco Ibanez
1920 *The Man of the Forest*, Zane Grey
1921 *Main Street*, Sinclair Lewis
1922 *If Winter Comes*, A.S.M. Hutchinson
1923 *Black Oxen*, Gertrude Atherton
1924 *So Big* (Pulitzer Prize), Edna Ferber
1925 *Soundings*, A. Hamilton Gibbs
1926 *The Private Life of Helen of Troy*, John Erskine
1927 *Elmer Gantry*, Sinclair Lewis
1928 *The Bridge of San Luis Rey* (Pulitzer Prize), Thornton Wilder
1929 *All Quiet on the Western Front* (German), Erich M. Remarque
1930 *Cimarron*, Edna Ferber
1931 *The Good Earth*, Pearl Buck
1932 *The Good Earth* (Pulitzer Prize), Pearl Buck
1933 *Anthony Adverse*, Hervey Allen
1934 *Anthony Adverse*, Hervey Allen
1935 *Green Light*, Lloyd C. Douglas
1936 *Gone with the Wind*, Margaret Mitchell
1937 *Gone with the Wind* (Pulitzer Prize), Margaret Mitchell
1938 *The Yearling* (Pulitzer Prize), Marjorie Kinnan Rawlings
1939 *The Grapes of Wrath* (Pulitzer Prize), John Steinbeck
1940 *How Green Was My Valley*, Richard Llewellyn
1941 *The Keys of the Kingdom*, A.J. Cronin
1942 *The Song of Bernadette*, (German) Franz Werfel
1943 *The Robe*, Lloyd C. Douglas
1944 *Strange Fruit*, Lillian Smith
1945 *Forever Amber*, Kathleen Windsor
1946 *The King's General*, Daphne du Maurier
1947 *The Miracle of the Bells*, Russell Janney
1948 *The Big Fisherman*, Lloyd C. Douglas
1949 *The Egyptian* (Finnish), Mika Waltari
1950 *The Cardinal*, Henry Morton Robinson
1951 *From Here to Eternity*, James Jones
1952 *The Silver Chalice*, Thomas B. Costain
1953 *The Robe* (new edition, see 1943), Lloyd C. Douglas
1954 *Not as a Stranger*, Morton Thompson
1955 *Marjorie Morningstar*, Herman Wouk
1956 *Don't Go Near the Water*, William Brinkley
1957 *By Love Possessed*, James Gould Cozzens
1958 *Doctor Zhivago* (Russian), Boris Pasternak
1959 *Exodus*, Leon Uris
1960 *Advise and Consent* (Pulitzer Prize), Allen Drury

1961 *The Agony and the Ecstasy*, Irving Stone
1962 *Ship of Fools*, Katherine Ann Porter
1963 *The Shoes of the Fisherman*, Morris L. West
1964 *The Spy Who Came in from the Cold*, John LeCarré
1965 *The Source*, James Michener
1966 *Valley of the Dolls*, Jacqueline Susanne
1967 *The Arrangement*, Elia Kazan
1968 *Airport*, Arthur Hailey
1969 *Portnoy's Complaint*, Philip Roth
1970 *Love Story*, Erich Segal
1971 *Wheels*, Arthur Hailey
1972 *Jonathan Livingston Seagull*, Richard Bach
1973 *Jonathan Livingston Seagull*, Richard Bach
1974 *Centennial*, James Michener
1975 *Ragtime*, E.L. Doctorow
1976 *Trinity*, Leon Uris
1977 *Silmarillion*, J.R.R. Tolkien
1978 *Chesapeake*, James Michener
1979 *The Matarese Circle*, Robert Ludlum
1980 *The Covenant*, James Michener
1981 *Noble House*, James Clavell
1982 *E.T., The Extraterrestrial Storybook*, William Kotzwinkle
1983 *Return of the Jedi Storybook*, Joan D. Vinge
1984 *The Talisman*, Stephen King and Peter Straub
1985 *The Mammoth Hunters*, Jean M. Auel
1986 *It*, Stephen King
1987 *The Tommyknockers*, Stephen King
1988 *The Cardinal of the Kremlin*, Tom Clancy
1989 *Clear and Present Danger*, Tom Clancy
1990 *The Plains of Passage*, Jean M. Auel
1991 *Scarlett*, Alexandra Ripley
1992 *Dolores Claiborne*, Stephen King
1993 *The Bridges of Madison County*, Robert James Waller
1994 *The Chamber*, John Grisham
1995 *The Rainmaker*, John Grisham

The *Bowker Annual* (New Providence, NJ: R.R. Bowker) is a massive tome published annually which contains practically every datum concerning the publishing industry, including exhaustive material on the best sellers for each year.

The #1 *New York Times Best Seller* (Berkeley: The Ten Speed Press) by John Bear is a mine of information. It is described (1992) as "Intriguing facts about the 484 books that have been #1 New York Times bestsellers since the first list in 1942."

Frank Luther Mott's *Golden Multitudes* (New York: Macmillan, 1947) lists best sellers since earliest Colonial days. It is a scholarly yet easily read history of the best seller phenomenon. Mott presents a rich anecdotal history as well as a wealth of professional and statistical data.[9]

Obviously, being a best seller for a year or two does not qualify a book for the ranks of the all-time best sellers. In fact, a book can be on the list of all-time best sellers without having ever been a best seller in any given year. Some books are enormously popular for a season and rapidly fade from public acclaim. Many of the best selling authors of this century have been utterly forgotten, as you may have observed in perusing the list.

Other books maintain a sustained popularity over the years that accounts for their great sales figures. One factor involved in the long-sustained sales strength is that of a book's being required reading by generations of students throughout the country. Something that really boosts book sales is the production of a great movie which has been based on the book. The most obvious example of that is *Gone with the Wind.*

Best sellers are sometimes enduring gems of literary art *(Doctor Zhivago)* but more frequently they seem to be of rather ephemeral interest *(Love Story, Valley of the Dolls,* etc.), not exactly milestones in the evolution of literature. Occasionally, they are Pulitzer Prize winners, but that is another story in itself.

---

[9]For a more modern book about best sellers, see Karen and Barbara Hinckley, *American Bestsellers* (Bloomington: Indiana University Press, 1989).

LITERARY PRIZES

SINCE THERE IS such a multitude of literary prizes—the National Book Award, the best children's books, the best science fiction, biography, history, drama, regional, etc., this discussion will be limited to the most famous.

First, the Nobel Prize. It would be frustrating to make a collection of Nobel Prize winners because the award is made to an author for his entire life's work. So a collector would have to collect all of the first editions of each Nobel author (a matter of hundreds of books) or he would have to collect perhaps one book of each author. Then the question becomes, which one?

Whether valid or not, the consensus of opinion, at least among the public, is that the Nobel Prize is always awarded to the best writer in the world as based upon the writer's entire canon. Even a superficial perusal of the list of Nobel winners will indicate that the assumption is asinine. The Nobel Prize was instituted for literature in 1901. Mark Twain was around nine years until his death in 1910. He did not receive it. Jack London didn't get it; he died in 1916. Nor did Theodore Dreiser, Edna Ferber, Edith Wharton, D.H. Lawrence, Willa Cather, Robert Frost, Arthur Miller, Norman Mailer, John Updike, James Michener or many other seemingly deserving writers. On the other hand, many of the awards were made to authors who were hardly known outside their own villages and whose work hardly made a ripple. How could the Nobel Prize people pass over James Joyce and nominate Grazia Deledda? More recently, there have been Nobelists created apparently because it was simply the politically correct thing to do.

Although we may wag our shaggy heads at the mysterious ways of the Nobel committee, as book collectors we can't ignore the phenomenon. When a great author such as Churchill, Steinbeck, Faulkner or Hemingway receives the Prize, it almost always increases the value of that writer's already published books. It is an awesome award even if it is capriciously bestowed.

NOBEL PRIZE FOR LITERATURE RECIPIENTS

1901 Rene F.A. Sully Prudhomme, France
1902 Theodor Mommsen, Germany
1903 Bjomsterne Bjornson, Norway
1904 Frederic Mistral, France
      Jose Echegaray, Spain
1905 Henryk Seinkiewicz, Poland
1906 Giosue Carducci, Italy
1907 Rudyard Kipling, Britain
1908 Rudolf C. Eucken, Germany
1909 Selma Lagerlof, Sweden
1910 Paul J.L. Heyse, Germany
1911 Maurice Maeterlinck, Belgium
1912 Gerhart Hauptmann, Germany
1913 Rabindranath Tagore, India
1915 Romain Rolland, France
1916 Verner von Heidenstam, Sweden
1917 Karl A. Gjellerup, Denmark
      Henrik Pontoppidan, Denmark
1919 Carl F. G. Spitteler, Switzerland
1920 Knut Hamsun, Norway
1921 Anatole France, France
1922 Jacinto Benavente, Spain
1923 William Butler Yeats, Ireland
1924 Wladyslaw S. Reymont, Poland
1925 George Bernard Shaw, Britain
1926 Grazia Deledda, Italy
1927 Henri Bergson, France

1928 Sigrid Undset, Norway
1929 Thomas Mann, Germany
1930 Sinclair Lewis, United States
1931 Erik A. Karlfeldt, Sweden
1932 John Galsworthy, Britain
1933 Ivan A. Bunin, France
1934 Luigi Pirandello, Italy
1936 Eugene O'Neill, United States
1937 Roger Martin du Gard, France
1938 Pearl S. Buck, United States
1939 Frans E. Sillanpaa, Finland
1944 Johannes V. Jensen, Denmark
1945 Gabriela Mistral, Chile
1946 Herman Hesse, Switzerland
1947 Andre Gide, France
1948 T.S. Eliot, Britain
1949 William Faulkner, United States
1950 Bertrand Russell, Britain
1951 Par F. Lagerkvist, Sweden
1952 Francois Mauriac, France
1953 Sir Winston Churchill, Britain
1954 Ernest Hemingway, United States
1955 Halldor K. Laxness, Iceland
1956 Juan Ramon Jimenez, United States (Puerto Rico)
1957 Albert Camus, France
1958 Boris Pasternak, U.S.S.R (prize declined)
1959 Salvatore Quasimodo, Italy
1960 Saint-John Perse, France
1961 Ivo Andric, Yugoslavia
1962 John Steinbeck, United States
1963 Giorgos Seferis, Greece
1964 Jean Paul Sartre, France (prize declined)
1965 Mikhail Sholokhov, U.S.S.R.
1966 Samuel Joseph Agnon, Israel
       Nelly Sachs, Sweden
1967 Miguel Angel Asturias, Guatemala
1968 Yasunari Kawabata, Japan
1969 Samuel Beckett, Ireland
1970 Aleksandr I. Solzhenitsyn, U.S.S.R.
1971 Pablo Neruda, Chile
1972 Heinrich Boll, Germany
1973 Patrick White, Australia
1974 Eyvvind Johnson, Sweden

Harry Edmund Martinson, Sweden
1975 Eugenio Montale, Italy
1976 Saul Bellow, United States
1977 Vicente Aleixandre, Spain
1978 Isaac B. Singer, United States
1979 Odysseus Elytis, Greece
1980 Czeslaw Milosz, United States
1981 Elias Canetti, Bulgaria
1982 Gabriel Garcia Marquez, Columbia
1983 William Golding, England
1984 Jaroslav Seifert, Czechoslovakia
1985 Claude Simon, France
1986 Wole Soyinka, Nigeria
1987 Joseph Brodsky, United States
1988 Naguib Mahfouz, Egypt
1989 Camilio Jose Cela, Spain
1990 Octavia Paz, Mexico
1991 Nadine Gordimer, South Africa
1992 Derek Wolcott, Trinidad
1993 Toni Morrison, United States
1994 Kenzaburo Oe, Japan
1995 Seamus Heaney, Ireland
1996 Wislawa Szymborska, Poland

The other literary prize discussed in this necessarily limited discourse is the Pulitzer. Established in 1918 by the famed New York publisher, Joseph Pulitzer, the prize is awarded in the following categories:

Fiction: For fiction in book form by an American author, preferably dealing with American life.

Drama: For an American play, preferably original and dealing with American life.

History: For a book on the history of the United States

Biography: For a distinguished biography or autobiography by an American author, preferably on an American subject.

American Poetry: Before the prize was established in 1922, awards were made from gifts provided by the Poetry Society.

General Non-Fiction: For the best book by an American not eligible in any other category.

Remaining consistent with our purpose of collecting—primarily—modern fiction, only the fiction Pulitzers will be listed. Complete listing of all the other categories are published annually by the *World Almanac*.

PULITZER PRIZES FOR LITERATURE

1918 Ernest Poole, *His Family*
1919 Booth Tarkington, *The Magnificent Ambersons*
1921 Edith Wharton, *The Age of Innocence*
1922 Booth Tarkington, *Alice Adams*
1923 Willa Cather, *One of Ours*
1924 Margaret Wilson, *The Able McLaughlins*
1925 Edna Ferber, *So Big*
1926 Sinclair Lewis, *Arrowsmith* (refused prize)
1927 Louis Bromfield, *Early Autumn*
1928 Thornton Wilder, *Bridge of San Luis Rey*
1929 Julia M. Peterkin, *Scarlet Sister Mary*
1930 Oliver LaFarge, *Laughing Boy*
1931 Margaret Ayer Barnes, *Years of Grace*
1932 Pearl S. Buck, *The Good Earth*
1933 T. S. Stribling, *The Store*
1934 Caroline Miller, *Lamb in His Bosom*
1935 Josephine W. Johnson, *Now in November*
1936 Harold L. Davis, *Honey in the Horn*
1937 Margaret Mitchell, *Gone With the Wind*
1938 John P. Marquand, *The Late George Apley*
1939 Marjorie Kinnan Rawlings, *The Yearling*
1940 John Steinbeck, *The Grapes of Wrath*
1942 Ellen Gasgow, *In This Our Life*
1943 Upton Sinclair, *Dragon's Teeth*
1944 Martin Flavin, *Journey in the Dark*
1945 John Hersey, *A Bell for Adano*
1947 Robert Penn Warren, *All the King's Men*
1948 James A. Michener, *Tales of the South Pacific*
1949 James Gould Cozzens, *Guard of Honor*
1950 A. B. Guthrie Jr., *The Way West*
1951 Conrad Richter, *The Town*
1952 Herman Wouk, *The Caine Mutiny*
1953 Ernest Hemingway, *The Old Man and the Sea*
1955 William Faulkner, *A Fable*
1956 Mackinlay Kantor, *Andersonville*
1958 James Agee, *A Death in the Family*
1959 Robert Lewis Taylor, *The Travels of Jaimie McPheeters*
1960 Allen Drury, *Advise and Consent*
1961 Harper Lee, *To Kill a Mockingbird*
1962 Edwin O'Connor, *The Edge of Sadness*
1963 William Faulkner, *The Reivers*

1965 Shirley Ann Grau, *The Keepers of the House*
1966 Katherine Anne Porter, *Collected Stories of Katherine Anne Porter*
1967 Bernard Malamud, *The Fixer*
1968 William Styron, *The Confessions of Nat Turner*
1969 N. Scott Momaday, *House Made of Dawn*
1970 Jean Stafford, *Collected Stories*
1972 Wallace Stegner, *Angle of Repose*
1973 Eudora Welty, *The Optimist's Daughter*
1975 Michael Shaara, *The Killer Angels*
1976 Saul Bellow, *Humboldt's Gift*
1978 James Alan McPherson, *Elbow Room*
1979 John Cheever, *The Collected Stories*
1980 Norman Mailer, *Executioner's Song*
1981 John Kennedy Toole, *A Confederation of Dunces*
1982 John Updike, *Rabbit is Rich*
1983 Alice Walker, *The Color Purple*
1984 William Kennedy, *Ironweed*
1985 Alison Lurie, *Foreign Affairs*
1986 Larry McMurtry, *Lonesome Dove*
1987 Peter Taylor, *A Summons to Memphis*
1988 Toni Morrison, *Beloved*
1989 Anne Tyler, *Breathing Lessons*
1990 Oscar Hijeulos, *The Mambo Kings Play Songs of Love*
1991 John Updike, *Rabbit at Rest*
1992 Jane Smiley, *A Thousand Acres*
1993 Robert Olen Butler, *A Good Scent from a Strange Mountain*
1994 E. Annie Proulx, *The Shipping News*
1995 Carol Shields, *The Stone Diaries*
1996 Richard Ford, *Independence Day*
1997 Steven Millhauser, *Martin Dressler: The Tale of an American Dreamer*

One of the most astonishing features of the Pulitzer Prize awards is the wonderful randomness of the selections. Several years ago, I determined to read each of the Pulitzer novels. I never found and have never seen a copy of anything ever written by Ernest Poole. Many of the Pulitzer recipients virtually vanished from history. Whatever happened to Margaret Wilson (1924), Margaret Ayer Barnes (1931), T.S. Stribling (1933), Caroline Miller (1934), Josephine W. Johnson (1935) and Harold L. Davis (1936)? And where were William Faulkner, Ernest Hemingway and John O'Hara during the 1930s?

I am sorry to say that my ambition was thwarted but not before I read 26 of the 76. Collecting the first editions of all the Pulitzer Prize fiction books would be a challenge. Many of them, such as *The Grapes of Wrath* and *Gone with the Wind*, would be very expensive. Reading the Pulitzers would be a great roller coaster ride through American literature. Since I only have 50 more to read...

You may have observed another interesting phenomenon regarding the Pulitzers, to wit: The Prize is often awarded for a novel that is clearly not one of the author's better works. Willa Cather wrote at least two (*My Antonia* and *Death Comes for the Archbishop*) books superior to *One of Ours* (1923). Neither of Faulkner's Pulitzer novels, *A Fable* (1955) nor *The Reivers* (1963) compare to *Light in August* or *Absalom, Absalom*—just to mention two.

Sinclair Lewis refused the Pulitzer in 1926 (*Arrowsmith*) because he had already been passed over when he had written better books, *Main Stree*t and *Babbitt*.

Even so, the Pulitzer committee, as you can see from the list yourself, is often right on the right book. Besides the obviously good choices (*The Good Earth, To Kill a Mockingbird, The Yearling*, etc.), sometimes the committee really does the right thing in awarding the Prize to a writer of sterling quality who has somehow not received the recognition of his or her more flamboyant peers. Such I believe to be the case of Wallace Stegner. His very first book, *Remembering Laughter* (Boston: Little, Brown, 1937) was every bit as wonderful as Ethan Frome, of which it was vaguely reminiscent. For the next 35 years, Stegner continued to write good books but it wasn't until 1972 that he won the Pulitzer Prize for *Angle of Repose*. Strangely, no movie was ever made from any of his books. As an American writer, he led an unusual life. He had an earned Ph.D. (Iowa), taught at Wisconsin, Harvard, and at Stanford, where he established the Stanford creative writing program, which he managed for more than 20 years. Some of his students were Dennis Murphy (*The Sergeant*), Eugene Burdick, Larry McMurtry, Ken Kesey, and many others. His own son, Page Stegner, is a successful writer himself.

Dr. Stegner had no divorces, no scandals, no drug or booze problems. He was a man of honor and decency all his long life (1909-1993). He paid his bills and kept his promises. Now what kind of a writer is that? We Americans are not accustomed to public figures of that stature.

Diane Peterson of Menlo Park, Calif. wrote a catalog of Stegner's publications. As a dealer's book catalog, it is a valuable work of scholarship for the Stegner collector.

The bibliography of Stegner was done by Nancy Colberg in the American Authors Series: *Wallace Stegner, a Descriptive Bibliography* (Lewiston, ID: Confluence Press, 1990), 270 pp. plus index. The introduction by James R. Hepworth is a gem of scholarship.

Recently in teaching a section on contemporary American writers, I compiled a hand-out for the class which was a list of a mere 100 authors. There were hundreds more. So to receive the Pulitzer Prize, however mysterious the choice, is still a tremendous honor. Besides the always-welcome money award, the Pulitzer is a sort of credential, a certificate of one's distinction as an author. It is very useful in selling one's further work, in negotiating contracts and in book promotion. It is analogous to a baseball player's MVP award.

FOREIGN LANGUAGE EDITIONS

MOST SUCCESSFUL AND popular authors will have been translated into many foreign languages. Early in our literary history Washington Irving, Fenimore Cooper, Poe, Hawthorne, et al. were translated into most of the European languages and into many exotic tongues as well. In modern times, renowned writers such as Michener, Styron and Herman Wouk may have 30 or more foreign language translations. Imagine the variables and permutations of attempting a complete collection of a world famous author.

Unless you are a fluent reader in other languages, it is advisable to limit your collecting to English language editions. Consider that your author has published thirty titles and has been translated into thirty languages. Nine hundred first editions! The first Albanian, the first Amharic, the first Armenian and so on to the first Yoruba and the first Zulu.

Furthermore, how would you determine whether a Basque or Bengali publication were a first printing or merely some reprint? Would you be willing to settle for a book club edition in Tamil or Laotian or Maori? Even with international computer access, such a collection would be impossibly unwieldy.

There are reasonable goals for foreign language collections, however. Suppose you are perfectly competent in Spanish like Ernesto Alejandro, the noted Michener collector. You might work at a collection of first editions from different Spanish speaking countries—the Mexican first, the Cuban, the Venezuelan, Peruvian, etc.

One might collect a single title in different languages. An Iranian friend used to collect every edition in every language he could find of the *The Rubaiyat* of Omar Khayyam, whom he fancied as an ancestor. He must have books enough to fill an airplane hangar by now. Since he was fluent in four European languages, Farsi, Arabic and Hebrew, he had an enormous advantage over most of us bibliomaniacs.

In these days (late 1990s) of relatively inexpensive world travel, especially with scholarships, fellowships and student exchange programs, the collection of foreign-language editions of your favorite author becomes quite feasible. Most academicians, intellectuals and assorted bookworms will have acquired at least a reading acquaintance with some foreign language(s). Interest in Asian languages is burgeoning, probably accelerated by immigration and the increasing role of Asians in world affairs. The Japanese, for example, have translated virtually everything of merit (and much besides) ever published in English. A reading knowledge of Japanese would open a whole world of books to the collector. Cities such as Tokyo, Osaka, Kobe and Fukuoka would be book-hunters' paradises. Japan may very well be the most book-friendly and literate nation in the world.

People in the armed services serving abroad should have access to the bookstalls of many other countries. If you have friends or relatives overseas with the military you might want to alert them to look for the books you want.

If your father is an airline pilot or your wife a flight engineer, foreign travel may be as routine to you as getting a haircut, in which case, you can shop for yourself.

Book dealers in other countries are very good about shipping your books home for you so that you don't have to carry them around with you. Most countries have special rates for the mailing of books so postage is not very expensive.

One of the most interesting features of a foreign language collection is the study of translations of poetry and fiction. Scholarly
treatises, textbooks and reference books seldom require more than
one good translation. Factual data is relatively easy to transfer
from one language to another. It is a different matter with creative
literature. The use of a Volkische or regional dialect may be nearly
impossible to render in another language. In reading the German
language edition of *The Grapes of Wrath,* the rendition of the
"Okie" dialect of American English is sometimes hilarious where
it is not supposed to be funny.

Poetry particularly often eludes the most conscientious transla-
tors. Bayard Taylor (1825-1878) employed his linguistic genius to
translate *Faust* from German to English when at least 15 translations already existed.

In a scholarly study of a literary work of great significance, the
study of translations can be critical in expanding one's understanding. The most obvious case is that of the Old Testament of
the Bible. Originally written in ancient Hebrew (except for a few
lines in Daniel in Aramaic), it was translated into the Greek of the
Septuagint about 300 B.C. It was then rendered into the Latin
Vulgate by St. Jerome (340?-420 A.D.) about 380 A.D. In 1384 John
Wycliffe produced a Middle English version directly from the
Latin. About 1525, William Tynedale made his wonderfully poetic
translation which constitutes about 30 percent of the diction of the
incomparable King James Version of 1611. After Tynedale was
brutally executed on orders of Henry VIII in 1536, an English
translation was authorized and was accomplished by Miles
Coverdale in 1539. Many other translations followed in the 16th
century, among which was the first Bible to be arranged by chapters and verses. That was the Geneva Bible of 1560 which was
produced by English exiles in Switzerland who had escaped the
wrath of Catholic Bloody Mary (1553-1558). The Authorized
Version of 1611 was supposed to settle the problem of accurate
and final translation of the Word of God but there have been
"improved" translations produced in practically every generation
since.

Besides English, there is the Great Cymric (Welsh) Bible of 1588
(antedating the A.V.) by William Morgan. You may not be aware

that there were 20 German translations before the definitive one by Martin Luther (1483-1547). A Basque Bible was in print in 1545. A Catalan Bible had been printed in 1478 (only 12 years after the Gutenberg Latin Bible) and Stephen Arndes printed a Low German Bible in 1594. A Dutch Old Testament had been published in 1477.

Returning momentarily to the matter of best sellers; the Bible is beyond comparison. It is easy here to quote from a good authority:

> *No one really knows how many copies of the Bible have been printed, sold or distributed. The Bible Society's attempt to calculate the number printed between 1816 and 1975 produced the figure 2,458,000,000 (2,458 x 10⁶). A more recent survey up to 1992 put it closer to 6,000,000,000 in 2,000 languages and dialects. Whatever the precise figure, it is by far the best-selling book of all time.*[10]

Complex printing histories and translations exist with the great secular classics—Homer, the Greek dramatists, Aristotle, Virgil, Dante and many others. In more modern times, such international literary treasures as *Don Quixote, Faust,* and *Paradise Lost* comprise a formidable challenge with their many translations. It has been said that there is really no such thing as a translation (in perfect exactitude) of a work of literary art. There are only versions. In the case of superlative translations, it is possible that the translator must have been about as gifted as the original author. Perhaps John Ciardi was inspired with an intimate muse when he put the terza rima of *The Divine Comedy* into modern English. Edward Fitzgerald may have even surpassed the son of the Tent Maker himself when he translated *The Rubaiyat* into English quatrains.

In collecting, the editions of other English-speaking countries—U.K., Canada, New Zealand, Australia, etc.—present an interesting facet of bibliophilia. They are "foreign" editions, yet they are in English. Many American authors are published in other English-speaking countries so that the first English, the first Australian and the first Canadian editions may become prized additions to your library.

---

[10]Russell Ash, *The Top Ten of Everything* (London: Dorling-Kindersley, 1994). p. 124.

We should distinguish between foreign editions and pirated editions. This was mentioned in the chapter "First Editions" but perhaps deserves a little elaboration here. Foreign editions are technically reprints for which legitimate arrangements for publication have been made. Pirated books are those that have simply been printed illegally without arrangements at all. Because of the enforcement of the copyright laws, pirating of books is rarely done in the same country in which the book was first published. Most pirated books are produced in countries that have little respect for international law, copyright or otherwise.

All of the pirated books that I have seen in the past 25 years have originated in countries employing the Chinese ideographic system of printing. Since the pirated books are reproduced photographically, the copyright data in the copied book is exactly the same as the original.

The pirated edition is usually smaller in size. It will typically have the same pagination but with reduced type size and margins. The dust jacket will resemble the original but will be poorly reproduced and ill-fitting. Another characteristic of the pirated book is that the paper is usually some photo-sensitive stock that has a peculiar slick surface. Another clue is that the binding is usually radically different from that of the American product. A pirated book is a counterfeit book, and like counterfeit money, it is illegal to import them into this country. The more you know about illegal imports, the more likely you will boycott them.

BOOK CLUB EDITIONS

TO MOST DEALERS and collectors, book club editions are weeds in the field of book-collecting. They are, like weeds, enormously abundant, almost valueless, and often tricky to identify. They are, with the more meticulous bibliophile, cordially hated and reviled. With ordinary readers and book buyers, book clubs are often suspected and distrusted.

There seems to be little justification for either of these hostile attitudes. Perhaps a brief argument for the book clubs is in order. Certainly they appear to be here to stay and we should learn to live with them, the more congenially the better.

First of all, few if any of the antiquarian book stores stock book club editions at all. Hence the sophisticated collector who patronizes such stores doesn't have to be concerned with them. Secondly, book club editions are readily identified by the knowledgeable collector and the likelihood of a bibliosavant mistaking one for a first edition is quite remote.

In identifying book club editions, look at the lower right corner on the back cover (binding, not dust jacket). If there is a small blind stamping (it can vary in shape), you have a book club edition (BCE). The stamping will occasionally be inked in color as with the BCE of *Travels with Charley*. Even more obviously identified, many BCEs will have "Book Club Edition" printed right on the front flap of the dust jacket. Most of them are so blatantly cheaper in binding, size, paper and printing that one can hardly confuse them with first editions. If he has seen and handled the first edition, the collector is not likely to mistake a BCE for a first— whether in a Salvation Army store, at a garage sale or in an upscale antiquarian bookstore.

It is a standard practice of publishers to print the retail price of a book on the inside front flap of the dust jacket. BCEs usually do not have those prices printed. However, many misguided bookstore clerks have the bad habit of clipping the price off of the dust jacket, thus depriving the bibliophile of a clue. Sometimes publishers will sell the rights to book clubs simultaneously with the issue of the first edition, and the BCE is very similar. Such is the case with Joseph Wambaugh's first book, *The New Centurions* and such is the case with Barbara Tuchman's *The Guns of August*. The only point of identification is the inconspicuous little indentation on the back board as described above. However, collectors are by nature nit-picky and it is not common for them to be fooled with BCEs.

The term "book club" in this context refers to the marketing practice of offering books to member subscribers at discounted prices. There are mystery book clubs, military book clubs, the History Book Club, Doubleday, Literary Guild, etc. The largest and best known is the Book of the Month Club (Camp Hill, Penn. 17012). As a working example, let us consider the Book of the Month Club (BOMC).

The BOMC was organized in 1926 and in May of that year issued its first book to 4,750 members. The book was Sylvia Townsend Warner's *Lolly Willowes*. In the nearly 70 years since, the BOMC has sold billions of books and has become the nation's leading bookstore, albeit a mail-order bookstore. The method of operation of other book clubs is comparable and the following observations will apply to them as well.

Book clubs can be a means of building a sound practical library (as contrasted to a bibliophilic collection). With bonus credits, often obtained by signing up your friends as members, you can obtain many books which might otherwise be hard to afford. For example, members have been able to acquire the 11 volumes of

Will Durant's *The Story of Civilization* quite inexpensively. Many good reference books and nice sets have been made available through the use of various marketing incentives.

An interesting feature of the BOMC is that it publishes monthly bulletins and catalogs of available books. The club often employs some of the best literary people in the country to write descriptions and reviews and thus you can stay abreast of contemporary publications.

The BOMC[11] has had a remarkable record for more than half a century of picking winners, i.e., best sellers and keepers. They have to, to stay in business. Their judgment has been at least as good as that of the Pulitzer Prize committee. Their choices may reveal much about the collectibility of authors. Nothing is certain in horse racing, weather forecasting or book collecting, but if the BOMC picks up a book, you may have a significant clue.

Most books sold through the book clubs are special printing— BCEs—and they are less expensive to manufacture and are distributed in large numbers. Hence they cost less than the publishers' editions. I know of no book clubs nowadays that sell publishers' editions. The History Book Club used to do so but it is a subsidiary of the BOMC now. So do not assume that just because you get a book hot off the press through your book club that you are getting a first edition. You might also consider what kind of a bargain you are getting after you have paid "shipping and handling" charges.

The usual method of operation of a book club is that the customer gets three or four books of his choice for a nominal sum as an incentive for joining. He may get $50 worth of books for enrolling. He is then obligated to buy, say, four books during the first year, after which he is free to discontinue his membership. That is a minimum of one book every three months. Nothing could be more reasonable. Book clubs provide reading copies at reduced prices and thereby serve a worthy purpose.

Book club editions are not spurned by all collectors. If you wish to assemble an exhaustive collection of an author, you may want

---

[11]For a splendid book about the BOMC, check out *The Book of the Month, Sixty Years of Books in American Life*, edited by Al Silverman (Boston: Little, Brown, 1986). 324 pp. plus index.

first impressions of all the reprints as well as the first editions. In a complete collection, the BCEs are part of the collection, too. They are part of the challenge. Finding a mint copy in dust jacket of a BCE of *The Winter of Our Discontent* may be quite as difficult as finding a first.

The United States has no monopoly on book clubs. In England, the Companion Book Club, the Folio Society and the Reprint Society of London have been around for decades and their editions of your author's works could be unusual additions to your collection. Book clubs exist in most of the countries.

Furthermore, the BOMC has a pro bono publico policy. They provide members books from time to time simply because it is a good thing to do. One such book was the poignant *One Day in the Life of Ivan Denisovich*. That one gift of the BOMC may have done more for the reputation of Aleksandr Solzhenitsin in this country than any other event.

Understand that one is never obligated to buy the book of the month. One may purchase one or more of several other selections or may choose not to buy any book at all. With most clubs you must remember to send back the little form that you receive with your monthly bulletin or the current selection will be sent automatically.

The book clubs of America have done much to improve reading and general literacy. English teachers can tell you that any organization that does that cannot be all bad.

AUTOGRAPHS AND INSCRIPTIONS

I had no objection at all
To selling my household effects at auction
On the village square.
It gave my beloved flock the chance
To get something which had belonged to me
For a memorial.
But that trunk which was struck off
To Burchard the grog-keeper!
Did you know it contained the manuscripts
Of a lifetime of sermons?
And he burned them as waste paper.

—Rev. Abner Peet
From *The Spoon River Anthology*
by Edgar Lee Masters

HOW MUCH MORE meaningful to the collector it is to have something personal of that friend and benefactor, the author. His autograph or inscription is perhaps the ideal symbol of the good author-reader relationship. Emerson once said that talent alone cannot make a writer; there must be a man behind the book. Study of the man, his life and his personality is an important element of the author collection.

Entirely aside from the intangible personal satisfaction of possessing the autographed copy, there is the crass commercial factor of monetary value. For example, a fine first edition of *The Grapes of Wrath* is worth about $1,000. With the author's signature, it is worth perhaps $1,500. Inscribed with a few words of greeting, it could be worth $2,000. Inscribed to a well-known person, who knows? It would depend upon who that person was and when the inscription was done and under what circumstances. There is a reprint of *The Grapes of Wrath* in the Sandburg Collection at the University of Illinois in Champaign-Urbana that is inscribed something like: "To Carl Sandburg—on the occasion of a good horseshoe game, from which he still owes me 35 cents." Signed: John Steinbeck. Only an auction could determine the value of such a unique gem.

An autograph is simply the signature of the author. It certainly raises the value and desirability of a book, but if the author signed a lot of books, the autographed copy is not unique. It may not even be scarce. If a writer has signed most of the copies of a first printing, the unsigned copies may be the scarce ones.

When Adrian Goldstone[12] had his great Faulkner collection, he was asked to lend his copy of *A Marble Faun* (a small book of poetry, Faulkner's first book, extremely rare). A great university was having a special exhibition of the works of Faulkner and made the request of Mr. Goldstone. Adrian replied that, of course, he would be glad to lend his copy for the exhibition, but why his? Surely the university had a copy of this little rarity. The curator explained that his (Goldstone's) was the only copy known which was not inscribed.[13] As such, it was a surpassingly rare curiosity.

Autographs and inscriptions are also subject to the inexorable laws of supply and demand.

---

[12]Co-author with W. Sweet of the Arthur Machen bibliography, co-author with John Payne of the Steinbeck bibliography (Austin: University of Texas Press, 1974). Goldstone was an ardent collector for more than 60 years. He died in June 1977.

[13]Probably the only copy known to him. However, Warren Howell told me that his firm, John Howell Books of San Francisco had handled two copies of *The Marble Faun* which were not signed. By the way, Allen and Patricia Ahearn in *Collected Books* (1991) indicate the value of *The Marble Faun* to be $20,000. And what if it were inscribed to Sherwood Anderson?

An inscribed book, as contrasted with an autographed book, is one in which the author has written some personal message, perhaps using the name of the recipient. That book is unique. There are no others with that inscription. If you have an opportunity to have a book signed by the author, ask him or her to write some little message or note and have him use your name in the inscription. If you can push your luck, get him to write the place and date as well. Wallace Stegner inscribed all of my first editions of his books, thereby making each one unique.

Autographs constitute another reason for collecting the works of living authors. There is always the possibility of meeting the writer and getting him or her to inscribe your books. That wonderful young author, Barbara Kingsolver, is also an entertaining and humorous public speaker. At her talks, she is generous with her time in signing copies of her books. At the risk of encouraging the "autograph hound" syndrome, let me just mention that attending presentations by authors can add another dimension to your collection.[14]

You can associate with people whose interests are similar to and supportive of your own. In many communities, there are library associations, "Friends of the Library" organizations, literary societies and book collectors' clubs. Membership in such groups naturally includes librarians, professors, writers, editors, publishers, book dealers and many others with intense interest and expertise in books. You can learn from them and through their friendship, you can meet other people, ad infinitum.

When Stephen Birmingham was in our community (Los Altos, Calif.), a literary friend invited me to attend a lunch with him at the Los Altos Country Club. It was an unforgettable experience and the author cheerfully inscribed my copies of *Our Crowd, The Right People, Real Lace,* etc. Such associations are much more fun than merely buying inscribed copies of collectible books—even if one can afford them.

---

[14]For instance, Prof. Barbara McNary of CSU Fresno once attended a talk by Amy Tan and the author inscribed the professor's new first printing of *The Joy Luck Club.* In just a few minutes, her copy was changed from being a good book to becoming an heirloom and a joy forever.

Ordinarily you need not feel that you are bothering authors to ask them to sign your copies of their books. It is people like us who buy their books and make them rich and famous. Writers know that and appreciate it. They are pleased to take a moment and sign books. But use common sense. If you recognize an author in a restaurant, it is ill-advised to interrupt him during his meal. Once John Steinbeck entered a restaurant in San Francisco and was recognized by the head waiter. "For God's sake, don't turn me in!" he pleaded. Writers and other celebrities need their peace and privacy as much as you and I do.

And the preacher said, "To everything there is a season and a time to every purpose under heaven."

There is another dimension to the matter of autographs and inscriptions that may never have occurred to you. Many books mention other people or contain contributions by others—such as forewords and introductions. Books often have dedications. They sometimes have illustrations. It is fun to get autographs of those people either in addition to or instead of the author. Who knows? The contributor of the foreword or perhaps the illustrator may be or may become more famous than the author. In my own book, *Books and Collectors* (Los Altos: The Book Nest, 1980), Warren Howell wrote the foreword and the great watercolorist, Edward D. "Rusty" Walker, Ph.D., did the illustrations.

If any of the characters in a book are real persons and are still living, it is interesting to get them to sign in the margins where they are mentioned. My copy of *The Log of the Sea of Cortez* is not signed by Steinbeck but it is autographed by many of the crew of the Western Flyer from the voyage to the Sea of Cortez in 1940. It even has the signature of the photographer, George Robinson, who shot the picture of Ed Ricketts that appeared in the book.

On the occasion of the first-day sales of the Steinbeck postage stamp, there was a celebration at the Salinas Public Library. John IV gave a talk and the author's older sister, Beth, was there. I had a copy of Steinbeck's *Life in Letters* with me and I asked Beth to sign in the margin on one of the pages where her letters appeared. She said to me, "Young man, don't you know you will ruin that book by having people write in it?" I also managed to get Dook Sheffield (lifelong friend and correspondent of Steinbeck's) and

Toby Street (also lifelong friend and lawyer) and several others to help me "ruin" that book. It was first inscribed by Elaine, Steinbeck's widow, who had co-edited the book with Robert Wallsten. Now it is one of my most prized possessions. I wouldn't trade it for a Rolex.

I have elaborated upon this theme somewhat to stress the point that there are many permutations and ramifications of the world's greatest hobby. All you need for acquiring fine first editions is money, but there is a lot more to the game than that.

Care, Handling and Condition

We all know that books burn—but we have the greater knowledge that books cannot be killed by fire.
— Franklin D. Roosevelt

CERTAINLY ROOSEVELT WAS right if we refer to the essence, the soul, the ideas of a book. But individual copies cannot only die by fire but by drowning, bodily trauma, loss and exposure. To the collector, condition is not just important; condition is everything. Books are not unique in this respect. Collectors of other things, such as coins, stamps, bottles, guns, art, glass, brass—in short, everything—demand top condition in their acquisitions.

One of the most famous of 20th century collectors, Morris L. Parrish,[15] had a reputation in the book world for his insistence upon immaculate condition in his books. He would not permit a book upon the premises unless it were virtually mint in all respects. Once "Parrish Condition" was an adjectival phrase among book collectors. It is a standard which most serious collectors emulate.

---

[15]The Morris Longstreth Parrish Collection is now at the Princeton University Library.

Condition is absolutely critical in ascertaining the value of a book. Fastidious collectors will usually emphatically reject a book in poor condition at any price. They just do not want it cluttering up their libraries, no matter how cheap. One time there were two copies of *For Whom the Bell Tolls*. One was a first edition in "good" condition with no dust jacket[16] priced at $20. The other was a "very fine" first edition in the first state dust jacket. The price? $500.

It is practically impossible to exaggerate the importance of condition in book collecting. From the beginning of your experience with it, make every effort to obtain books in the best possible condition. This is another advantage of collecting living authors. You can get their first editions new as they are published.

Incidentally, many authors are published in first limited editions, commonly signed. Then the first trade edition is produced. With prolific authors, this factor makes all the difference. Perhaps the best example is James Michener. Michener is so prolific (39 books at last count) and so popular (see any list of best sellers) that the limited editions are about the only ones that are really collectible. Except for his early books (*Tales of the South Pacific* is extremely rare), nearly all of his titles (*The Source, Hawaii, Alaska, Texas, Poland, Space*, etc.) have been published in enormous numbers. Therefore, the first trade editions are plentiful. It is the limited editions, which are rarely seen for sale in used bookstores, that are scarce, sought after, and expensive. The great bibliophile T.H. "Jake" Jacoway of Palatka, Fla. (Gen. Joseph Stillwell's hometown) is possibly the premiere Michener collector. He tells me that it is necessary to make arrangements with a really competent bookseller in order to acquire the limited editions upon publication.

Another prince of Michener collectors is Dr. Michael J. Quigley (see his chapter in this book) of Athens, Tex. Quigley was an old friend and travel companion of Michener and had nearly all of his collection signed by the author. He confirmed what Jacoway says about the limited editions.

---

[16]With this book, the dust jacket must be present to identify the first state. In the first state dust jacket, there is no photographer's credit below the author's picture on the back panel of the dust jacket. Later states credit Arnold, the photographer.

The classification of books by their physical condition may be reviewed using the following guide:

I. *"Mint." As new.* Self-explanatory. Rarely or never used. Some books are bought new for the express purpose of becoming collector's items, the same as with stamps and coins. This practice is particularly true with fine press books. Mint condition books will have no marks or damage whatever. In fact, some of the old letterpress books remain "uncut," i.e., the edges of the pages have not been separated. The books have never been read.

II. *"Very fine"* is a term applied to used books just slightly below Category I. Some catalogs use the term "near mint," which is about the same. This grade of book may have been read, may have a little discoloration or light scuffing to the dust jacket.

III. *"Fine"* is somewhat less "fine" than "very fine." Most "fine" books have been used but they are bright, clean and undamaged. The have been cared for. Dust jackets may be a bit chipped or split and catalogs will usually mention anything like that. The majority of the stock in a good used bookstore will fall into this category.

IV. *"Very good"* books will be tight, clean and generally respectable, but more scuffing, minor lesions, fading and signs of use appear.

V. *"Good"* books are about as low of a rating as the traffic will bear in dealing with modern books. This merely means that the book will have all pages intact, will be reasonably tight and serviceable. Such books are entirely adequate for all purposes except that of the fastidious collector.

You must not expect such a general classification system to be more than a rough guide. The classifying will vary with the dealer or collector who may vary in his criteria from ultra finicky to downright liberal. His motive, too, may influence his standards. You would be astonished at how criteria can change from the position of seller to that of buyer.

Catalog descriptions will usually include pertinent data beyond simple classification of condition. If a book has a former owner's name, stamp, or bookplate, such information will normally be indicated. "Hinge starting" or "Page 324 slightly torn" are common remarks found in conscientiously prepared catalogs.

Beware of "else fine." One catalog description: "Spine stunned, some browning, light foxing, name in ink on flyleaf, some underlining, a few dog-eared pages, title page missing. Pages 12 and 123 repaired. Else fine." Else fine? What else is there? Even so, in the case of an extremely rare book, copies of which simply don't exist in good condition, this could be, for somebody, a very tempting entry.

There are many variables involved in the consideration of the condition of books. It is unreasonable to expect an 18th century seven-volume novel to be as "fine" as a collectible modern edition. Consider the age of books when applying any system of classification. Another thing: "Good" copies signed or inscribed or with highly desirable provenance will nearly always be worth more than merely "mint" copies. If a rough old copy of *The Descent of Man* has the handwritten note: "Property of Robert G. Ingersoll,[17] Dobbs Ferry, New York, August 11, 1893" and below that, the bookplate of Karl Menninger, M.D. of Topeka, Kan., do not discard. Do not donate to charity. Do not hold out for a better copy.

If you notice shaggy old books in the library of a bibliophile renowned for his "Parrish" syndrome, you can be pretty sure that they are very special, perhaps inscribed copies or association copies like the Darwin book cited.

I have a (merely) fine first edition of Irving Stone's *Clarence Darrow for the Defense,* but tipped in is a cancelled check written by Darrow in 1921. The book was published in 1941. Who knows when the check was added to the book? At any rate, it makes the book much more interesting and valuable than any mint copy.

There are books that for all practical purposes are simply unobtainable in "fine" or better condition. Collectors of the *McGuffey Readers* realize that those books were used by schoolchildren and that "fine" copies are out of the question. This is the usual case

---

[17]Ingersoll (Aug. 11, 1833-July 19, 1899), Civil War colonel, attorney, orator, the Great Agnostic, had the best library of skeptical books in the country. Once asked what it had cost him, he replied that it had cost him the governorship of Illinois, a seat in Congress and possibly the presidency of the United States.

with dictionaries, children's books and textbooks. It also applies with nearly equal force to mystery and detective fiction. People "read them to death" and leave them in poor condition, if they survive at all. Mint condition paperback collectible books are difficult to find, too.

THE DUST JACKET

Regarding the bibliophile and the dust jacket. It must be understood that the dust jacket is an integral part of the book. In the bibliophilic world, the book is simply incomplete without the paper jacket in which it was published. Of course, some books are published without jackets but they are usually works such as textbooks or books in special leather bindings. However, a book that was originally issued in a dust jacket is virtually disqualified as a collector's item if the jacket is missing. Unless it is surpassingly rare, the careful collector will not even possess a book without the dust jacket. If a book is inscribed or has a particularly desirable provenance, a collector might condescend to shelve it similar to the case of books in poor condition. If originally equipped with a jacket, the collector will not be satisfied until he has obtained it. It is a common practice for a collector to buy a copy of a book he already has merely to obtain the jacket. Often he will buy another copy to get a better dust jacket, thereby upgrading his collection. Typically, the bibliophile will be constantly upgrading his library, replacing "good" copies with "fine" ones and "fine" ones with "very fine" copies. He will strive to obtain jackets for his books that lack them and to get better dust jackets for those books that have merely "good" ones.

In November 1832, Longmans of London issued an annual with the title, *The Keepsake*. This is the first book known to have been published with a dust wrapper (as a dust jacket is called in Britain). The wrapper was light buff with a decorative border in red which enclosed the title. It had advertisements for other Longmans publications on the back. It had long been accepted that the earliest dust wrapper was issued in 1862, but in 1934, John Carter of London discovered the unique Longmans book. In 1952, while being transported to the Bodleian Library at Oxford, it was lost and no other copy has ever been found.

The first pictorial dust jacket was also produced by Longmans. It was fitted to an edition of *Pilgrim's Progress* of 1860. The illustration on the jacket was a woodcut by Charles Bennett which was also printed in the book itself.[18]

Dust jackets have become increasingly popular, particularly since World War I, so that today it is exceptional for a book to be issued without one. Whatever you do, never discard or destroy a dust jacket, not even on a book that may seem worthless trivia to you. It might be collectible for someone else. As in the antique business, one man's junk is another man's treasure.

With many collections it is desirable to have a copy of all of the variants, states, etc. of every edition. In such collections, the first variant of the first state of the first printing of the first edition is merely the core book of the collection of that title. Important and desirable to an expanded collection of this sort are the first printings of the Triangle Books, Tower Books, Grosset & Dunlap reprints, Sun Dial Press, Modern Library Editions, Collier reprints, book club editions and condensed or abridged editions. Finding fine copies of those books in their dust jackets is not as easy as you might surmise. After all, who cherishes and preserves cheap reprints for decades? It may well be that a fine copy of the first Modern Library edition[19] (in original dust jacket) of *In Dubious Battle* would be harder to find than the first (Covici-Friede) edition itself. It would cost only a fraction of the price of the publisher's first edition, but try to find it.

You may be looking for a particular book someday and if you find it lacking the jacket, you may be inclined to impugn the ancestry of the unknown person who, sometime in the past, disposed of it. It might have been Steinbeck:

> *I myself am a hater of jackets. My impulse is to get them off and throw them away quickly. They crease and get in*

---

[18]Patrick Robinson, *The Book of Firsts* (London: Rainbird Reference Books, Ltd., 1973). p. 26.

[19]The "first" of the Modern Library must so state: "First Modern Library Edition" on the copyright page. Modern Library books do not indicate "Second printing" or "Third impression" or have any other clues about the issue. Reprints simply omit "First Modern Library Edition."

the way...Does the jacket contribute anything to a book beyond adding to the cost? It would be interesting to see.[20]

This is a common attitude but in spite of our veneration of the great novelist (all of whose first trade editions were issued in dust jackets), we must not emulate him in this respect. We must not ruin the value of a book by rendering it incomplete. It is imperative that we keep in mind that for bibliophilic purposes, the dust jacket is part of the book. Do not tear out the illustrations. Do not rip out the frontispiece. Do not dispose of the dust jacket.

As a matter of fact, the dust jacket does contribute considerably to a book besides adding to its cost. Many dust jackets have pictures of the author, usually on the back panel, which do not appear in the book itself. Dust jackets often have a checklist of those works already published by the author—sometimes a very helpful feature to have. Dust jacket flaps often have a synopsis or précis of the book covered by the jacket. All of which is in addition to the obvious function of protecting the book from dust, damage, sunlight or moisture. We have all had the experience of removing a dirty, old, faded jacket to find the book itself in bright, beautiful condition.

No matter how absurd the dust jacket question may seem to you, it is advisable to be aware of this factor from the first. If you derive nothing else from this book than an awareness of the dust jacket fetish, then you did not waste the price of the purchase nor the time in reading it. If you are going to play the game, you must follow the rules, and the bibliophilic rules insist that the original dust jacket accompany the book with which it was published. Facsimiles don't count.

Since dust jackets are merely paper, it is extremely difficult to keep them in perfect condition. There are two ways to protect and preserve them. The first—highly recommended—is to cover each jacket with a clear plastic cover designed for the purpose. Libraries make extensive use of such covers but they are not usually stocked by bookstores, office supply or stationery stores. Unless you can find a store that handles them, you will have to order them from

---

[20]Ray Freiman, ed., *The Author Looks at Format* (s.l., the American Institute of Graphic Arts, 1951). p. 30.

the manufacturer. One source of adjustable book jacket covers is: Bro-Dart, 1609 Memorial Ave., Williamsport, PA 17705.

The 10-inch adjustable covers will fit most of your books and, excepting the big "coffee-table" type books, the 12-inch size will fit the rest. Librarians use such plastic covers and they can show you how to fit them. It is not difficult but must be done carefully.

Another way to preserve dust jackets is to remove the jackets, lay them out flat and store them in a cool, dry place. Some book lovers prefer the appearance of books without their jackets. Many books are beautifully bound and their owners are reluctant to hide such binding under paper dust jackets, many of which are themselves gaudy, dull or otherwise unattractive. But, of course, most books are not bought as collector's items in the first place and little thought is given to their preservation. Hence the relative rarity of used books in "very fine" condition.

A veteran book dealer told me a story about the practice of storing dust jackets. The bookseller is sometimes called upon to make appraisals of libraries for probate or insurance purposes. In the course of helping to settle the estate of a book collector, the appraiser examined the library and found most of the volumes to be first editions in fine condition, but all of them were lacking the dust jackets. As he was about to conclude his appraisal and call it a day, he said, half to himself, that it was certainly regrettable that such fine books were without jackets. Then the widow of the departed bibliophile explained that her late husband had always kept the jackets in a drawer of a large armoire. Going to a massive old mahogany masterpiece, she disclosed the jackets stored there in as pristine condition as the day they were laid away. The dealer had to do his appraisal all over again, as in most cases the jackets multiplied the value of the books many times.

It is almost beyond belief and if it were not easily demonstrated, I would hesitate to relate the strange fact: The jacket is often worth more than the book. In fact, with really collectible books, the jacket is nearly always worth more. A case in point: A fine copy of *The Grapes of Wrath*, first edition, no jacket, is worth about $100—if you can find a buyer. The same book in a fine original dust jacket is worth $1,000. And you can find a dozen buyers within hours.

Besides the aesthetic value of having a complete thing and gratifying the collector's mania, dust jackets sometimes determine the "state" or "printing" of a book. As we have seen, this is true of *For Whom the Bell Tolls*. It is also true of Wolfe's *Look Homeward, Angel*, which must have the author's photograph on the back panel. I once bought a copy of Edward Sapir's *Language*. The title page and copyright page both indicated "1921," the year the book was first published. I found no evidence that it was a reprint until I examined the dust jacket, whereupon I discovered advertisements for books published in the late 1930s.

Dust jackets are commonly found torn, split, chipped, perforated, gouged, wrinkled, soiled, water spotted, sun faded or in any combination of these conditions. It would be so nice to always have them in mint condition, but with scarce collectible books, we often have to settle for what is available, particularly with a limited budget. Obviously, nobody prefers a "restored" or repaired dust jacket but such a wrapper is better than none at all. Perhaps it is better to have one neatly repaired than hanging in shreds or pieces.

Dust wrappers, however badly mangled and mutilated, can often be salvaged or improved to an astonishing degree. You may want to improve the condition of your jackets. Practice on some expendable jacketed books. Buy some book club editions of romance novels at the Goodwill store to practice on. Try this: Lay the jacket out flat on a smooth, clean dry surface. Flatten the creases and wrinkles as much as possible with repeated strokes with the fingers. Running a straightedge over the jacket may help. Smooth out any wrinkled or bunched up places and salvage any torn or loose pieces.

Then place acid-free white paper tape along the margins on the reverse side of the dust jacket. Do not use any other kind of tape. No masking tape or drafting tape and absolutely no transparent tape of any kind should ever be used on jackets.

Most of the damage to jackets will be to the horizontal margins and most of that will be to the top margins. Make sure that the tape itself is smooth and flat. The sticky side of the tape will show through any holes or places where the original material is chipped away but it will be library white and relatively inconspicuous and unobjectionable. NEVER, never put any kind of tape on the front or printed side of the jacket. The white paper tape will show through holes and chips. That is unavoidable. But anything on the face of the jacket will look tacky. Never use transparent tape in the same room with a dust jacket; it may somehow manage to stick to it. Such tape will always be of a different texture or different refraction from the material of the jacket. It will glisten in the light and will emphasize the patched-up appearance of a repaired jacket. The idea is to keep the jacket together and serviceable and yet make it look as nearly original as humanly possible. Transparent tape defeats the purpose.

I must inform you that many professional book experts would be appalled at my advising amateurs in the matter of "doctoring" book jackets. If you have any reservations about "messing around" with repairs or "appearance augmentation," don't get into it. Some considerable skill, patience and diligence are necessary. These are well-intentioned suggestions that I have found to work very well. However, such little jobs can be botched or overdone.

Next, if we are to continue, examine the face of the jacket and determine if any of the cracked or scuffed places can be touched up. If so, use a calligraphy pen of a matching color to restore the finish. Very dark intense colors respond quite well but weak reds, pale yellows and oranges and greens are nearly impossible to match. Fortunately, black is the most common color in dust jackets and the covers of paperback books and it is the easiest to touch up. Pale shades are best left untouched.

The same techniques can be used with excellent results on the covers of paperback books. White-line creasing on paperbacks can be virtually eliminated.

Much of the soiling of dust jackets and paperbacks can be removed by simply erasing it. Use a soft pink or gum eraser to avoid abrading the paper. Proceed cautiously to avoid wrinkling or bunching the paper. The light colored areas, especially white, can be dramatically brightened by erasing away the dirt and smudges. In the case of jackets or paperback covers with slick non-porous surfaces (coated stock), soiling can be removed by applying a clean cloth dampened with a liquid household cleanser. Then apply a vinyl polish and you will find that the cover looks new. This treatment not only removes the surface scum and dirt but leaves the coated stock looking bright and shiny. Such an application helps to prevent future soiling and discoloration.

Never use any form of moisture on porous or coarse-textured paper surfaces. It will soak in and probably leave a stain.

After taping the back side of the dust jacket, carefully and minimally to hide holes, repair chips and prevent further deterioration, and after restoring the color and cleaning away the soil, cover the jacket with a clear plastic cover. Because of their reflective and refractive properties, plastic covers have an astonishing ability to minimize defects in your dust jackets. The entire effect is that of making your jacketed books much brighter and handsomer in appearance.[21]

GENERAL CARE OF BOOKS

Do not "dog-ear" pages to mark your place. The resultant crease will permanently diminish the appearance and value of the volume so abused. Don't use letter openers, pens, pencils, knives, crayons, pieces of chalk, jack handles or pipe wrenches to keep your place. Use cards—business cards, file cards, ordinary old playing cards (jacks or better?) all work fine and they do not distort your books or leave tracks in them. You should not use the flaps of dust jackets to mark your place either. It damages the jackets by distorting and creasing them. Avoid leaving anything like flowers, leaves or newspaper clippings in books. Such material is certain to discolor the pages it comes into contact with. Newspaper paper is so acidic that it will quickly discolor the pages it lies between. If you must keep a newspaper clipping with a book, put it in a plastic folder. Even an ordinary envelope is much better than the naked newsprint.

Don't write in or underline books. This admonition doesn't apply to cheap working copies, reprints or textbooks (which will probably be obsolete next semester anyway) or generally expendable books. Such advice is subjective but you may agree that it

---

[21]For an entire book on the subject of dust jackets, see the wonderful work by Stephen Heller, *Jackets Required* (Chronicle Books, 1995).

makes sense. In any event, it is to be questioned whether there is any value in marking up a book of any description. Years ago there was an essay in some freshman English "reader" titled "How to Mark a Book." I had my doubts even then. Maybe it's all right, but where do you draw the line? A much better idea is to keep 3x5 cards to make notes on. Even the college bookstore doesn't want your trade-ins smeared with marking pens and writing.

If there is anything consistent about book collecting, it is inconsistency. It is clear that marking and underlining and writing in books ruins them as collectibles. Most bibliophiles simply will not have such a book no matter how cheaply it may be acquired. However, we again have the inevitable exception. If the marking or note making can be proved to be that of an author or another famous person, then such marking or note making can be very valuable indeed. So if you should find Newman Flower's *Handel* with Bruno Walter's notes in the margins, do not erase them. If you should observe Carl Sagan's notes in a copy of Sir James Jeans' *The Stars in Their Courses* (Cambridge: The University Press, 1931), acquire the book as nonchalantly as possible.

There is an old story (stories are only old if you have already heard them) about a man talking to a book dealer on the telephone. He is saying that he has an old Bible printed in a foreign language and it appears that some fool named Luther has been writing all over it. Could it be worth anything?

So any advice about marking books has to be subject to circumstances and tempered with a little mule sense. Horse sense is not good enough.

The ultimate rejoinder to any advice about the treatment of your books is that if you own them, they are your property to do with as you please. And if you want to make a paper doll out of the title page, that is your business. If you remove the steel engravings from a fine 19th century volume to decorate your bedroom, that is your affair. If you plan to keep a book all your life, then whatever you do with it is up to you and you cannot be expected to worry about it after you are gone. However, as you have loved and enjoyed your books, have a thought for those who will live after you. Someone in the past must have cared for the books that you now cherish. Someone, whose grandparents are not yet born, may someday rejoice to own the books that are now on your shelves. After all, do any of us ever really own anything? We are custodians for a little while and surrounded by a sleep.

If you have any inkling that you may someday want to sell your books, all or some of them, do not be astonished if no one wants them marked up, underlined, stained, broken, incomplete, dog-eared or without dust jackets.

BOOKPLATES

Book collectors are congenial people, but where there are two together, there are three opinions. Many suggestions in this book are subject to dispute and for nearly any statement that might be made, a vociferous opponent can be found. No matter how cautious a treatise might be, someone will find occasion to disagree with or dispute virtually every line.

Which brings us to the subject of the bookplate. Stationery stores encourage their use. Custom printers are in favor of them. Dealers and collectors tend to disdain them, unless they have belonged to someone famous. Book catalogs will often have a contemptuous little note such as "bookplate on flyleaf" when describing a listing, as if it were a flawed copy. It is clear that the dealer would cheerfully be rid of it and might even get a better price if the bookplate were gone.

On the other hand, bookplates add a distinctive personal touch to a book for the owner, especially if he has custom-made plates of his own. Plates identify the book and may serve to permit the owner to enter pertinent data, such as place and date acquired, price paid, etc.

Incidentally, you might consider devising a private code for listing the price you paid for each book in your collection, either on the bookplate or on the card in your file. You may, of course, arrange the same data in your computer storage. A simple code suffices if you do not wish it known what you have invested in your library. For example, use letters of the alphabet. Begin somewhere past the first letter (A=1 is too easy), as in, say, J=1, K=2, etc. Now suppose you paid $54 for a book. Your code would read: "NM." If you know any other alphabets—Greek, Hebrew, Arabic, Russian—your code would be so much the more effective. You won't baffle a cryptographer, but this method will suffice to conceal data from most of us. This will have no effect on the value of your books but it might help to decide whether you want to accept a given price or not.

Bookplates are a common feature of provenance. Provenance, you may recall, is anything of a personal nature added to the book which attests to the history of that individual volume. If former owners have been well known, provenance can add significantly to the value and interest of a book. Bookplates are perhaps the most common feature seen as evidence of former ownership. A physicist bibliophile is a collector of Michener and one of his most interesting items is a first edition of *Hawaii* that has the bookplate of "Kathy and Bing Crosby."

In my collection of Clarence Darrow, I have a first edition of Irving Stone's *Clarence Darrow for the Defense*. It has a tipped-in card signed by Stone and some tantalizing sort of provenance. Tipped in on a front leaf is a check signed by Darrow for $944.44, a substantial sum for that year, 1921. It is endorsed by the payee and canceled but I can learn nothing of the circumstances. Still, it makes for an interesting copy.

A rather mediocre copy of Frank Norris' *The Octopus* (worth $300 now in a fine first edition) in a reprint normally worth perhaps $20 was offered not so long ago for $100. All because it had the name "John Steinbeck" embossed on one of the flyleaves. Books having belonged to famous authors are particularly sought after by their collectors.

My copy of *To a God Unknown* (now in the Fukuoka University collection) had been a duplicate copy sold off by the University of Virginia library and was originally a part of the Clifton Waller Barrett collection. It still had the Barrett bookplate and the Virginia library receipt, thus making it a much more interesting copy than a merely fine first edition.

The fabulous Goldstone collections of Sinclair Lewis, William Faulkner, John Steinbeck, Agatha Christie and others have Goldstone's renowned "Mt. Tamalpais" bookplate. In my collection of Van Wyck Brooks, there is a fine advance review copy of *The Flowering of New England* with Goldstone's "Mt. Tam" bookplate.

Like so many other things in the world of book collecting, the decision to use bookplates is a matter of personal judgment and taste. If you prefer to use them, you might consider having plates made to your own design. Some people use the family coat of arms (Barrett) or the clan tartan. Goldstone used a geographical feature. Bookplates have a venerable, honorable and complex history, so you will be in good company if you choose to use them. Bookplates vary widely, from custom tooled leather to simple gummed paper. Their cost varies accordingly. Paper plates can be printed to your specifications at reasonable cost. Be sure to specify acid-free paper when ordering from a printer. Some paper contains acid (usually sulfuric) which will, in time, transfer a mirror image of itself to the page facing it. This is called "acid migration." Ungummed paper is to be preferred since gummed stock may cause the page to which it is applied to bunch up or become wrinkled around the bookplate. The plate should be attached with a thin coat of library paste. It is better to paste only the top of the bookplate for attachment thus making it much easier to remove at some later time.

Many librarians and curators advise against leather bookplates. The thicker leather plates impart a deforming effect to end-papers and the acid in the leather may have a damaging effect upon paper.

Address labels, such as those used on envelopes, and address stamps are adequate methods of identifying books. These are not as objectionable as some purists would have you think, as they can be easily covered by the bookplate of the new owner. Which brings up a good practical use of bookplates. They can be used to cover a multitude of unwanted writing or marking or imperfections. There is valuable provenance; then there is trash. Graffiti. Many books will have obscure names: "Bobby Smith's book" or unidentifiable presentations: "To Danny from Uncle Sid for Xmas." Some will have library stamps, name stamps, notes, price markings, imperfect erasures, etc. A good opaque bookplate of generous size, say, 3" x 5", will make a neat cover-up. Even if you have to use more than one bookplate, so what? They look better than the graffiti.

It is not to be inferred from the foregoing that everything except famous provenance is to be disdained. Many collectors cherish old signatures, notes and inscriptions. "For Angus MacKenzie—First Prize in Rhetoric—Wick School—May 24, 1928" is an inscription that may have a certain sentimental value to some bibliophile. It is all a matter of taste and preference.

The use of crayons to mark prices by Friends of the Library personnel in one community was initiated to frustrate the efforts of a book bootlegger. This person, a book scout and a shame to his kind, carried an eraser with him when attending book sales sponsored by the Friends. He would erase the prices marked in pencil with a view to saving a few cents on each purchase. So because of one jackal, everyone had to put up with crayon markings. The only thing that can be done with crayon is to cover it up. A good opaque bookplate will do.

CARE OF BINDING

There are all sorts of factors involved in "condition" of books— underlining, marking, writing, sun-fading, moisture damage, dirt and dust contamination, decomposition of paper (foxing and browning), heat warping, missing leaves, tears, dog-earing, herniating of unopened pages, wrinkling, etc. Damage to the binding is one of the most conspicuous and common defects. It is usually caused by physical pressure of some kind—dropping the book on the spine or edges, or having it struck by another object. If the book is loose, it can often be repaired by the careful injection of library glue. Simple firming up of a floppy old book can be done by anyone, but if a book is of great age and/or value or has complex damage, repairs should be done only by a professional. Of course, you should recognize that it would be better to avoid acquiring a loose copy in the first place.

Much can be done with a loose spine if it is not too far gone. In 1966, I arrived late for a Friends of the Library sale in Nevada City, Calif. and there wasn't much left. Neglected by everyone was a scruffy, loose old black leather copy of the 1860 edition of *Worcester's Unabridged Dictionary.* Joseph Emerson Worcester's. Not Webster's. It was the world's first illustrated dictionary and for many years was a very successful competitor of Webster. Worcester's company became defunct in the 19th century and remaining copies are collectors' items. The binding was faded, dry and scuffed. The spine was loose. It was almost beyond redemption, but much could be done toward restoring it. It had been made by craftsmen from fine materials. A thin application of glue reunited the backstrap and the spine and more was applied at strategic places throughout the book where the pages had pulled from the spine. The hinges were intact. The glue was spread neatly and all excess wiped away. The book was placed under a stack of heavy books and left to set overnight. The glue held, the spine and signatures aligned and to this day, the massive old tome is firm and functional. As for the leather cover, it was treated with a fine grade of paste leather polish. Applied just as you would to a boot, then buffed with a soft brush, the old leather fairly leaped to life. Even now, the 135-year-old black leather gleams on my shelf between the old tan *Webster's Unabridged* of 1857 and the 1822 red leather *History of Scotland.*

It is amazing to observe what can be done to restore the appearance of worn and tired books. Scuffed and faded hardback books can usually be rejuvenated with the careful application of ordinary paste leather polish of the appropriate color. If it's a blue book, use the blue polish. If green, use the green paste. Cobblers' shops and saddle shops stock leather polish in every color you are likely to need. Do not use the "cream" type. Use paste. Scuffed edges and corners of boards can be touched up with the skillful application of liquid leather dye. Of course, it must be done carefully and with the correct shade.

The paste or wax-type leather polish works beautifully with leather books as you might expect, but it will also restore the color and impart a shine to smooth-textured cloth hardback books. Proceed just as with leather. Do not use anything on suede or on fuzzy or porous textured covers.

I had thought that I had discovered this process from independent deduction and experiment, but I found that other collectors had been using this technique for years before I "discovered" it. Some of my old leather books have been polished and re-polished for twenty or thirty years and each time, they respond just like a fine boot or saddle.

Once the scuffed and faded areas have been covered and stained with a matching color of polish, the book can be brushed and buffed just like a shoe. The polish will brush right off of gold lettering, but avoid getting it on lettering that is merely inked. A blue book with white lettering would not be a good candidate for polishing.

Obviously, the texture and color, with varying degrees of fading, will differ from book to book. Experiment with some expendable books in order to get the feel of the process. With a little experience and practice, you can judge very well which color to use, how much and where.

Everyone who observes the operation is astonished at the startling and dramatic improvement that can be made in the appearance of books. The leather polish is not only harmless to your books, it is beneficial. It imparts color and protection to the faded and scuffed areas and renders surfaces resistant to moisture. After many years of shelf life, books can be polished again, but unless frequently handled, there is little need for further treatment. The natural oils and waxes of the polish also promote flexibility and resilience of hinges and spine and thereby reduce the danger of cracking and splitting.

There are special preparations used by library technicians and book binders that are excellent for leather but like saddle soap or clear wax, they will not impart color or cover scuffing.

If a book is indeed rare and valuable or if it has great sentimental value and is in an advanced state of dissolution, consider having it completely rebound. Your professional bookseller can advise you on how to make arrangements with a binder. You might take the book to him for advice. Book-binding varies enormously. There is utilitarian binding that is of minimal cost and there are bindings that are unique works of art that are, like other art forms, very expensive.

Consider this analogy: Spending $10,000 to restore a 1934 Ford five-window coupe would be a good investment. Spending a thousand dollars on an '86 Escort would be foolish.

Many excellent books provide extensive professional instruction and advice on the care of books. One of these is by Douglas Cockerell: *Bookbinding and the Care of Books*, a paperback published by Lyons & Burford, 320 pages. Another is *The Care of Fine Books* by Jane Greenfield, a Lyons & Burford paperback of 224 pages.

MORE ON HANDLING BOOKS

Bookkeeping taught in one lesson: Don't lend them.
— From a bookplate

ONE FAMOUS COLLECTOR sputters with indignation when telling how some of his guests get up from dinner and go right into the library and start looking at books. Always make sure that your hands are clean when handling books. It is painful to see a fine scarce volume (or any book for that matter) with fingerprints and smudges on it. The value of a book is severely reduced when it is degraded from "clean copy" to "soiled."

We are so accustomed to handling tough textbooks, telephone directories, dictionaries and encyclopedias that we easily become careless in the handling of all books. In dealing with old, rare, valuable books, we must keep in mind that we are handling treasures and that they are usually rather delicate. An example is my three-volume set of Chalmers' *Mary, Queen of Scots* (London: John Murray, 1822), octavo, half calf. Although more than 170 years old, the set is still sound and beautiful, the polished leather fairly glowing in the light. But we must handle such elderly friends with care. They are fragile and highly susceptible to damage.

When looking at a book, cradle the volume firmly in the left hand so that the pages can be turned and examined with the right. With Hebrew books, as well as some others that read right to left, hold the book in the right hand and handle pages with the left. Avoid opening the book to its maximum angle. Viewed at a minimum angle, the tightness and integrity of the binding will be preserved. Your bibliophile friends will be delighted to see you handling their prized possessions in such a thoughtful manner.

Move deliberately and cautiously at all times when handling collectibles of any kind, particularly old and delicate things. Sudden, spastic movements probably have caused as much damage to them as floods and earthquakes combined.

Arrange books on shelves closely but loosely with plenty of space between volumes. When removing a book from a shelf, grip the spine in the middle, lift up enough to clear the shelf surface and gently pull toward you. If the books are too tightly packed together, it isn't possible to get the fingers between the volumes. Then it is only natural to tip the book toward you by the top of the spine. That is how the very common splitting at the tops of spines occurs. Lift the book up and out without dragging its tail on the shelf. That is how the tails of spines get torn, chipped and split. Even if you have to take a volume out and lay it on top of a row of books, that is better than having them jammed too tightly together.

BOOKENDS

Avoid using bookends that have bases that protrude under the books. Sooner or later, the base will be driven into the side of a book. Most bookends of that type force the books to ride up on the base plate at a cramped angle. They are also awkward and inconvenient to use and cause the books that sit on the base to be somewhat higher than the rest of the volumes on the shelf. Such bookends are a chronic nuisance and you should avoid them like clichés.

Use bookends that are heavy and will not be easily scooted along the shelf by the pressure of the books they are supporting. They should remain firmly in place and keep the books from falling over. If you have a lapidary friend or access to a lapidary saw, you can make attractive bookends from rocks of high density.

Do not use light or porous stone. Avoid most sandstone as the stone tends to shed grains of sand. Among the very best is petrified wood. It is gorgeous, dense, heavy and can be had for something less than extortion. Marble, agate, alabaster—all are excellent.

Just saw the rocks so that one side—the one facing the books—is flat. From the shape of the rock, decide which is to be the base or bottom. Saw that surface flat so that the rock will stand up straight as a bookend. If you take some care to select a beautiful piece of stone and polish it out, your bookends can be veritable works of art. Any heavy material such as metal—copper, pewter, brass, bronze—can be made into beautiful and useful bookends at very little expense. Be sure to buff the burrs off any metal pieces because a rough one can scuff your books.

It is important to keep all of your books at sharp 90° angles from the surface on which they are placed. If they are allowed to lean, they may develop a permanent distortion or warp. Do not allow a book to lean and support the others. Large heavy books should be laid down flat instead of standing upright.

If you must smoke, smoke outside the library. You know how smoke accumulates as scum on the inside of the windows in a car? A similar process occurs in your library. It may take longer to become noticeable but the same thing happens. Never smoke while examining a book. All too often, ashes or even a live coal will fall, sometimes with disastrous results. Food, drink and tobacco should be avoided in the book room. Don't take any chances with wine glasses or coffee cups. The most careful and coordinated of us can occasionally slip and the sight of a fine book soaking up burgundy is something you may not be able to handle. If anything can possibly happen it will.

Glass paneled bookcases are the best, preferably with leaded panes and beveled edges in doors that lock. Unlocking the book-cases and swinging the doors open to your guests should at least impress them with the value that you place on your books and should encourage careful, even reverent handling. This type of bookcase almost eliminates the dust, smoke, moisture and other contaminants that threaten your books.

A most desirable book storage is the old-fashioned rotary book-case. Revolving bookcases are a delight and a convenience, store a lot of books in a small space and present a handsome appearance. Any reasonable price for such a piece of furniture is a bargain and with good care, will last indefinitely.

If you have a choice in the matter, try to select a room for your books that faces away from the sun—the north side of the building in northern latitudes. Better yet, a room with no windows at all would permit no sunlight on the books. If you cannot avoid having the sun shine on your books, cover them to prevent direct sunlight, which is sure to cause fading.

Heat is another enemy. Never place books near a stove, heating vent, clothes dryer, water heater or furnace. Store books in cool, dry places only. The great book palaces, the citadels of fabulous collections, such as the Humanities Research Center at the University of Texas, maintain rigid environmental control in book storage. The temperature and humidity are kept at ideal levels. As far as possible, go ye and do likewise.

BOOKS AS INVESTMENTS

Money and time are the heaviest burdens of life, and the unhappiest of all mortals are those who have more of either than they know how to use.

— Samuel Johnson, LLD.

ADRIAN GOLDSTONe (1897-1977) was one of the great book collectors of the world. Without people like him, antiquarian book dealers would simply be out of business. Mr. Goldstone was once asked if he had made money, lost money or had about broken even over the years. Without hesitation, he replied that he had made small fortunes on all his collections. Beginning in the late '20s, he unerringly collected winners—Hemingway, Faulkner, Sinclair Lewis, and later, Steinbeck. At his death, he had what was probably the finest collection of Agatha Christie in existence. And this is to mention only a few of his collections.

Goldstone would collect all of the limited editions, the first trade editions, special publications such as private printings, biographical and critical works of a particular author. When the collection was as nearly complete as he thought possible, it became what he called a "static" collection. At that point, he would become somewhat bored with it, sell it, and take up another collection objective.

It is, of course, still possible to collect the works of authors who are just emerging from obscurity. Many writers are rather well known but are perhaps in the early or middle phase of their careers. It is not uncommon for a great literary talent to produce thirty or more books. So if some admired author has published 10 good books and is only 40 years old, it is altogether probable that his best years may lie ahead of him. You may buy his first editions now and as they are published.

Purists such as Bob Fellman, the prince of Dickens collectors, insisted that one should collect the books he loves whether they turn out to be good investments or not. I heartily agree. Book collecting should be for love and pleasure. However, this chapter is on "Books as Investments" and I am determined to avoid too many digressions.

Even Goldstone had to start somewhere and at some time, just as we do. One possibility would be to collect a Pulitzer Prize winner. Literary prizes are certainly no guarantee of lasting literary excellence, but they indicate a possible starting point. Much the same might be said of the best sellers. It is a strange irony of our literary world that the terms "best seller" and "literary excellence" are sometimes incompatible. I never quite believed that. There are just too many exceptions—*The Good Earth, Gone with the Wind, The Yearling, Cannery Row* and so many others.

Any writer who is known to be a darling of the "Eastern Establishment" might very well be a good bet for collecting for investment. The "Eastern Establishment," very generally speaking, consists of the book reviewers of the big city newspapers and of the powerful weekly news magazines. The publishing industry of the U.S. has always been centered in New York City along with the review and criticism professions. In the "Establishment" are the English departments of the Ivy League universities, including Harvard, Yale, Brown, Dartmouth, Columbia, Cornell, Princeton and Penn.

The trouble with collecting the wonderful long-gone writers of the past is that their books are already in the collections of the universities, the big private and public libraries and in the collections of private individuals. When available at all, the old masterpiece first editions are so expensive that one has to tie up too much money in them and, except for normal inflation, they do not usually rise in value enough to be good investments. If they can be had cheaply (as in inheritance), then that is an altogether different matter.

In any event, the most gratifying of all collection themes is simply the one that appeals to you. If Michener is not exactly a darling of the Eastern Establishment, so sorry. If you love Michener through his books, collecting them would probably be a great joy. At this time (early 1997), he has published 38 books and he is 89 years old. The satisfaction of having read and enjoyed his books and of owning fine first editions of each title—that is the essence of bibliophilia, not buying books on speculation.

In the mid-'60s, I read Joseph Wambaugh's *The New Centurions*. Of the 13 books he has written since then, all have been best sellers and many of them have been made into movies. I had no idea whether his books would become collectors' items or not. I bought them in new first printings and greatly enjoyed every one of them. It is a pleasure just to have them—fine in dust jacket—whether they ever become valuable or not.

Much more important than financial growth potential is your own personal interest. Use your investment talent on stocks, bonds, livestock, real estate, etc. Collect books as a tranquil and comforting hobby. If your interest is in futuristic technology, cybernetics, aeronautics and international intrigue, collect Dean Ing.

There is nothing wrong with increasing one's worldly wealth, but surely book collecting should be a labor of love, a devotion, not a strategy for gain. Ideally, any hobby should promote halcyon days of the spirit, not compound stress by bringing the tension of the business world into the library.

The collecting of books should be a dedication to ideas and wisdom and the surrounding of oneself with the great and good works of the human mind. It should enrich and ennoble and educate. (Now don't change the subject by bringing up the collecting of comic books!)

Somehow there is something almost obscene in profiteering and trafficking in books by the bibliophile. However, as in every other aspect of life, ideals are hard to live by in the practical world. The Almighty Dollar, inflated as it is, is a ubiquitous feature of everyday existence. Bibliomaniacs tend to have spouses who do not have the same obsession. Collectors often have a dire need, sometimes desperate, to justify purchases whose expense surpasses the limits of common decency. It greatly facilitates domestic tranquillity to be able to demonstrate one's fiduciary acumen by reference to dealers' catalogs which show prices substantially in excess of the purchase in question. Thus the chronic preoccupation with money—like it or not. So, the "investment" factor cannot long be ignored or suppressed.

Like other addicts, the book maniac has to support his habit. In order to do that, he may have to do a little dealing himself. When bargains can be found, even if the material is entirely outside of his own collection interests, he can buy them and trade them for books he wants to keep. A certain collector of the books of John Muir found the very scarce first edition of *Tales of the South Pacific* and managed to trade it for two of the Muir books he had been looking for. Another collector, a woman who collects ethnic or sectarian cookbooks, found a Robinson Jeffers first edition, sold it and bought the cookbooks she wanted. By the way, her collection would interest anybody. She has Mennonite cookbooks, Mormon, Adventist, Cajun, Armenian, Greek, Gypsy, Czech—and many other such specialized food books.

But this is penny-ante stuff compared to the operations of the big league dealers and collectors. In the rarefied atmosphere occupied by bibliophiles George Ticknor and James Lenox of the 19th century, Morgan and Huntington of the early 20th, Jerome Kern, Jean Hersholdt and A. Edward Newton later in the century, only the rarest and costliest books elicit interest. Fortunes have been made and lost at those altitudes. Rare books have escalated in value better than most chattels. However, dealing on that level requires massive erudition, vast experience, talent, financial resources and a certain sense for which there is a good German word, *Fingerspitzengefuhl*—a feeling in the fingertips. That is for the past masters. This book is for the entered apprentices. We must all advance while becoming thoroughly familiar with the early degrees of our craft.

The amateur has no more business hunting for Paul Revere's "A Collection of Psalm Tunes" or a Bay Psalm Book than the neophyte in art has in shopping for a Rembrandt. Therefore, in our context, the word "investment" is used in its most immediate and practical sense. Where does the poor aspiring beginner begin? At the beginning.

By "poor" I do not mean indigent. I am not referring to inmates of institutions or welfare recipients or to the habitually unemployed. The "poor" I have in mind are those intelligent and discerning people of education (formal or otherwise) who have such obligations that their budgets do not permit indulgence in an expensive hobby. The peripatetic fruit picker or criminal fugitive is not apt to be reading this anyway.

With the development of the serious collector's zeal, there often develops another dimension to his financial thinking. He begins to think in terms of what books he could buy with the money available. He will find himself making sacrifices, substitutions and rationalizations. As the collector's mania progresses, priorities become shifted and mundane things such as groceries and rent become mere threats to the Collection.

In many respects, book collectors appear to be quite normal and resemble other members of the community. They have jobs, families and obligations much as everyone else. However, the Collection must be nourished and with all of those other demands upon his resources, the collector's craftiness and versatility often become honed to a high degree of virtuosity. If you think alcoholics deceptive and philanderers devious, for sheer subterfuge, smuggling and cover-up, I will pit an advanced bibliophile against the best sneaks available.

In one advanced case of bibliophilia, probably terminal, the collector worked out a system for getting books into the house. His library was on the second floor of an old Victorian and when he would go out book hunting, he would leave a length of cord hanging from his library window. When he would come home with some books, he would tie them to the cord, go nonchalantly upstairs and pull them up, hand over hand. One day his wife was sitting by the window downstairs sewing when some books went by. She just reached out with her pinking sheers and cut the cord. I never heard what happened after that and I don't want to think about it.

In contemplating further involvement in book collecting, the book lover must sort out his priorities. If cars, clothing, jewelry, furniture, entertainment, travel, etc. are more important to you than your library, you may have difficulty handling an obsession of this nature. Like any mistress, it is demanding. It requires sacrifices. An eminent Dickensian drove an old Chevy for years, which, if it were a book, would have been classed as "shaken." His neighbor drove an overpriced Teutonic Ostentation. Pickwick's attitude was: "Well, he has his collection of speeding tickets; I have my collection of Dickens."

Besides the books, there are other expenses in collecting. There is transportation and parking. You have to get around to bookstores, estate sales, library sales, flea markets, etc. There are telephone calls to dealers all over the country. Postage adds up, too. You will need to correspond with dealers, advertisers and other collectors. You will want to request catalogs, place ads and distribute want-lists, all of which must be figured into the expense of your avocation.

It must be repeated that the investment factor of book collecting should be a secondary consideration. Collect as a labor of love, a work of gratification and learning. If you collect first and limited editions, and when possible, get them signed and in fine condition, they will usually increase in value as the years pass. Even if they do not, well, that was not the purpose in the first place. My modest collection of books about Henry Ford and the Ford Motor Co. is not much more valuable than when I started it 20 years ago, but I cherish it just the same.

You should reflect, too, that you will probably never sell your collection anyway. Therefore, your money will be tied up in your library during your lifetime and it becomes a moot point whether it was a good investment or not. You will find that your books will be the cynosure of your life and your money has been invested in tranquillity, satisfaction, scholarship, and the sheer joy of owning something intrinsically worthwhile. *Ars est longa; vita brevis.*

Libraries and Collectors

*A large library is apt to distract rather than to instruct the learner;
it is much better to be confined to a few authors than to wander at
random over many.*

— Seneca

LIBRARIES CONSTITUTE THE collective memory of man. The essential factor that elevates Man above the most intelligent of other species is not only his use of language but the cumulative effect of his knowledge. Present day horses are no better informed than were the horses of ancient times, but we know more about physiology and anatomy than Hippocrates and more about mathematics than Eratosthenes. The libraries of the world are the extensions of the memories of the millions who have lived and died and their records and writings are available to the living. No lawyer can know all of the law, but he or she can find it in the law library.

Bibliophiles customarily have unbounded love, admiration and respect for libraries and librarians. In fact, many bibliophiles are librarians. However, the library can be the enemy of the collector, or at least a competitor of awesome size and power.

First of all, librarians utterly ruin books for collectors. Once the library gets through writing on the spines of books in that leprous white ink, pasting those paper card-pockets on the pastedown pages, stamping the library name all over the pages, perforating the illustrations and committing other assorted atrocities, Hell wouldn't have the books. An "ex-lib" note in a dealer's catalog is the kiss of death on the value of any book so assaulted. Unless, of course, it has been a pampered possession of the "Special Collections" (non-circulating) department. When the library sells off some of its old books or its duplicate copies, you may obtain reading copies cheaply, but they are ruined for the collector.

A case history: It was one of those books that was not especially rare or valuable but annoyingly hard to find in fine condition. It was *American Winners of the Nobel Literary Prize* edited by Warren French and Walter E. Kidd, published in 1968 by the University of Oklahoma Press. The copy I found had been an inmate of a county free library. It had a tenacious tag glued to the tail of the spine of the dust jacket. It had the plastic dust jacket cover taped to the binding. On the title page, it had a number stamped under the editors' names. Then it was stamped DIS-CARDED in blue ink right on the title page. A despoiled and ravaged book. I would have liked to have had it before it was arrested and punished.

The "ex-lib" element itself is a rather minor complaint, a small bone in the throat of the bibliophile. The real resentment he or she feels is in the taking out of circulation, often permanently, of vast numbers of collectible books. A not-too-hypothetical case: Old Professor Snarf has spent the spare time and devotion of the past 40 years in building his collection of early American literature. He has skipped many a lunch and has driven econo-box cars in order to afford the precious volumes that now insulate the walls of his house. The collection is the principal motive for his existence. He has had some of those books for more than 40 years. They are like having the spirits of Melville and Whitman, Longfellow and Lowell, Whittier, Holmes and Alcott with him in the evening of his life.

The lamb licks the hand of the butcher but the old professor has seen the ax from the first. He knows that there will be a disposal of his library. He recoils with horror when considering the crowds about the lawn on the day his possessions are auctioned off to strangers. His son cares nothing for books. And the names he loved to hear have been carved for many a year on the tomb. He can't sell the collection himself. What can he do?

He can will his library to his alma mater, or donate it to the college where he has taught for the past 20 years. Then the collection will be kept intact. It will preserve the name of the donor, however obscurely. It may even prove useful to a researcher someday. So the kindly old bibliophile goes to one cemetery and sends his books to another.

Never again will anyone know the thrill of finding, buying and owning any of those lovely old books. None will ever appear again in any book dealer's catalog. Nobody will ever make a profit from their sale and so pay wages, rent and make a living. They are out of circulation forever, for the library is a corporate body and is immortal. The individuals who staff the library pass on like the rest of us, but the institution continues and the books remain in special collections, embalmed, as it were, buried forever from bibliophiles, except for visiting privileges.

There are at least two sides to every argument and in all fairness, it should be mentioned that libraries preserve for the general public, or at least for those who are interested, collections that might otherwise disappear for decades in the private library of some collector where they would be available only to special guests. George R. Stewart called my attention to this:

> The only place, as far as I remember, in which I differ
> with you is on libraries. From a scholar's point of view,
> a book held by a collector really disappears.[22]

The curator of special collections at a major university agreed with Prof. Stewart:

> Books are not embalmed in special collections; they
> are still available to legitimate scholars. Also with
> microfilming, they are available not only to the library
> holding them, but everybody.[23]

But, of course, I am thinking like a collector, not a research scholar. Certainly, one can go to the special collections at San Diego State and use the wonderful collection of Henry James, but they always want their books back. San Jose State has an entire

---

[22]From a letter from George R. Stewart, late professor at U.C. Berkeley and author of many good books, including *Earth Abides*.

[23]From a conversation with the curator.

section of the library devoted to Steinbeck. The Steinbeck Research Center is a veritable museum and a library, but the collectors' items are not for sale.

The existence of this gentle competition between individual and institution should be known to the collector as he will encounter the phenomenon if he persists in his madness.

Perhaps more ways could be found to secure the return of books besides mutilating and defiling them. Surely in this age of electronic hypertechnology, miniaturization, and the advanced use of magnetism and chemistry, some wizard could devise a method whereby books are not ruined when they enlist in the service of libraries. They may be discharged and returned to civilian life someday.

The library is the heart of any institution of learning. It seems appropriate that the library at DeAnza College (one of the top community colleges in the world) is officially designated as the Learning Center. Library special collections are nearly always based upon what were once private collections. Names famous in the world of libraries—Morgan, Huntington, Bancroft, Bender, Houghton, Beinecke, Newberry, Clark, and many others—are those of individual collectors. Thus a rather benevolent symbiosis exists between the individual and the institution.

CONCERNING PUBLISHING COMPANIES

The public, with its mob yearning to be instructed, edified, and pulled by the nose, demands certainties...but there are no certainties.
— H.L. Mencken

LIKE OTHER BUSINESS enterprises, American houses (publishing companies are called "houses") usually find a niche and tend to specialize in certain types of books. If you learn some of the characteristics of the most frequently seen products of the major publishers, you can learn to evaluate a shelf of books rather more quickly than you could if you had to examine each volume.

It is not within our scope to list all of the publishers, foreign and domestic, defunct or thriving. There are thousands. Even so, a discussion of a few of the most frequently seen imprints might be helpful. The book hunter will rapidly develop this branch of collecting knowledge.

For instance, Grosset & Dunlap rarely publish an original manuscript. The majority of their publications are reprints. The Bobbsey Twins and Tom Swift books are exceptions. The business of G & D is publishing reprints—decent quality at low prices. So if you are looking for first editions of Jack London or John Steinbeck, forget the G & D publications. They are reprints.

The name of the publisher is usually at the tail of the spine. Some of the older reprint houses are difficult to evaluate as they were not lavish with publishing dates, copyright dates or prefatory material. Typical of these are late 19th and early 20th century books published by Crowell, A.L. Burt, Hurst (not Hearst), etc. You may find some useful and desirable books under those imprints, but rarely first printings. Knowing this can save you time. A little later in the 20th century, such publishers as Blue Ribbon Books, Sun Dial Press, Triangle Books and Modern Library Books are typical reprint houses. Some reprints are elegant and manufactured with fine craftsmanship. Typical of those are the Heritage Press books, the Folio Society (British) and the wonderful Everyman reprints.

Representative of the reference and textbook publishers are Silver Burdett, Science Research Associates, McGraw-Hill, Harcourt Brace (with various corporate name changes), Houghton Mifflin, Funk and Wagnalls, and William C. Brown. These do not produce text-type books exclusively but if your primary interest is fiction, these can usually be skipped over lightly.

Most of the universities publish books under their own imprints through the university presses. Some, such as the University of Indiana Press, have become rather distinguished in the publishing industry and even have overseas branches. As you might expect, most of the books produced by university presses are works of scholarship, as opposed to creative works of fiction, drama and poetry.

Viking Press and Macmillan are examples of enormous publishing houses which publish nearly every form of the printed word. One is apt to find virtually anything under those imprints so that any generalization would be risky. International publishing houses such as Macmillan produce books throughout the non-communist world. Publishing practices and traditions can vary with the part of the world in which the book is published.

If you know that Robert Frost's publisher was Henry Holt,[24] Van Wyck Brooks' was Dutton, Will Durant's was Simon & Schuster, then you know what to look for when searching cliffs of books for works of those writers. Many writers stay with a single

---

[24]Frost once called himself Holt's oldest employee.

publisher. We associate Hemingway with Scribners, Faulkner with Random House and Steinbeck with Viking (after 1937). Many writers have several different publishers during their careers. Mario Pei, late of Columbia University, had at least six publishers: Lippincott, John Day (Pearl Buck's husband and publisher), Random House, Hawthorne, Knopf and Funk and Wagnalls. Most of Dr. Pei's more than 40 books were on language and linguistics.

You can eliminate foreign editions if you are interested only in first editions. Suppose your author's first editions are published by Viking Press. The apparently first editions published by Heinemann are British editions. If you are collecting an author first published by Cassell, Ltd., London, then the Dodd Mead & Co. books are reprints—first American editions.

VANITY PRESS BOOKS

A vanity press book is one for which the author has paid all the expenses of publication himself just to get the book in print. Sometimes this is done by people who can afford to do it merely for the satisfaction of seeing their work in print. And that's the end of it.

Occasionally, however, a work of great merit will simply fail to gain acceptance by a publisher. In this case, if the author can raise the money, he may publish the book himself. If the book is a success, the author has a financial advantage because he stands to make all of the profit from the venture. Normally, the publishing company would make the majority of the profit and the author would be compensated with a very modest (commonly 15 percent of the wholesale price) percentage of the income from sales. Such a payment is known as a royalty.

Such a practice is understandably uncommon as few people who can write can also afford the expense of publication. Fewer still have the means to publicize and promote the book.

A famous example of a book that began with a commercial publisher (Doubleday) and then became a sort of vanity press book was *The Jungle* by Upton Sinclair. The first edition is a Doubleday publication (1906) and later editions are under the "Jungle Publishing Co." imprint.

FINE PRESS BOOKS

Fine press books, often simply called "press" books, are different from vanity press books and commercially produced books. The commercial publisher is a risk-taking, profit-making (hopefully), advertising, competing business enterprise. It will produce just as many books as it can sell, and no more—if it can help it. The publisher will undertake to produce and market only that material which, in the judgment of shrewd and experienced editors, will sell sufficiently well to return a reasonable profit—or even an outrageous profit, if possible. The company doesn't want to produce any more copies than it can sell because then there is the problem of disposal. What do we do with all these books that nobody seems to want?

The "press book," on the other hand, is usually produced as a work of art and a labor of love. Typically, a fine press book will have been printed with carefully chosen type on high-quality paper, perhaps handmade paper. The press book will have generous margins all around, carefully designed for balance and beauty. Illustrations are expected to be first-rate art and the book will be specially bound. The entire project may be carried out with little regard for the profit motive and it will be produced in limited numbers.[25] Thus the "fine press" book bears more resemblance to an art project than to a commercial publication.

The "small press" is not the same as the "fine press," even though small presses sometimes produce fine press books. The small press is to Macmillan as the mom & pop grocery store is to Safeway. Their basic structure, function and motive for existence is essentially the same. The great difference is their size and scope of operation. A contemporary example of very fine press work is that of the Yolla Bolly Press operated by Carolyn and James Robertson. A masterpiece of that press is a printing of Steinbeck's *Flight*, illustrated by Karen Wikstrom, with an afterword by Wallace Stegner, signed by Stegner and Wikstrom, 1984.

There are hundreds of small presses in America and there is a professional organization of people involved in the business. They have

---

[25]*How Edith McGilicuddy Met R.L.S.* was printed by Ed Grabhorn of San Francisco in 1942 for the Rowfant Club. This Steinbeck short story was printed in 152 copies. With the original glassine wrapper, it was worth $2,500 in 1995.

annual conferences and seminars and have a permanent place in the publishing industry. Fine presses, though, usually have a precarious grip on existence. They tend to come and go, often ceasing to exist with the death of their founders and guiding geniuses.

Publishing companies ordinarily do not own or operate the printing plants which physically manufacture their books. Nor do they own or operate the binderies. Printing and binding are separate functions not usually engaged in by publishers. The printing and binding industries have separate and distinct histories and structures. Commercial publishers, both the giant conglomerates and the small presses, "farm out" their printing and binding. Now this work is done by huge automated, computerized machines with a minimum of manual labor or craftsmanship. Fine press operations usually perform all functions. Typical of the older fine press imprints are Kelmscott, Doves, and Golden Cockerel. Of course, there are many others. There have been many superb fine press books made in France, Germany and Italy. In recent years, many fine books in European languages have been printed in Asia, particularly Hong Kong and Japan. But these are merely expensive, high-quality books, not really "fine press" books in our narrow definition. Other superb quality books are the Franklin Library and Easton Press products. Those, too, are high-priced, super-quality books that are produced in large numbers for wide distribution. They are not "fine press" books.

The Limited Editions Club has published many beautifully made and superbly illustrated books, often signed either by the author, the illustrator or both. My copy #13 of Van Wyck Brooks' *The Flowering of New England* is signed by both the author and the illustrator, R.J. Holden. It was published in 1941 in 1,500 numbered copies in slipcase. LEC books are a pleasure and a delight but they are not "fine press" books either.

Most of the great university "Special Collections" library departments have examples of gorgeous fine press work. A book like the Kelmscott Chaucer must be seen to be appreciated. There is a magnificent copy at the Bender Room, Green Library, Stanford University.

Dealing with the Dealer

I wonder what the Vintners buy
One half so precious as the stuff they sell.
                    — Omar Khayyam

In local directories, find the names, addresses and phone numbers of booksellers in your area. List the information in a personal notebook so that it will be convenient to use. Ask an ABAA member dealer (most dealers are members) for the free ABAA directory. Make it your business to call on the owners or managers personally and get to be friends with them. The professional (as opposed to a clock-watching clerk) is highly intelligent, incredibly well-informed and generally sensible. It is his business to handle your wants appropriately and to cultivate you as a long-term customer. The dealer who is not courteous and helpful, even to a novice, may risk losing a customer who would spend God-knows-how-much over a period of several years. It pays to be nice to people and most dealers know that and act upon it. Collectors can profit by being nice people, too.

It could not be stated better than when Adrian Goldstone drew upon his 60 years of experience as a collector and bibliographer:

I believe that book collecting, like almost everything
else in this world, is successful simply because of hard

*work. I haven't found tremendous success in buying
books by going into stores haphazardly and finding
things on their shelves...*

The calls, however, on booksellers are very valuable. If a book
dealer will know you as a person, rather than as a name, he will
remember you, and when something comes into his stock in
which you are particularly interested, he will offer it to someone
he knows as a flesh-and-blood person rather than just someone
with whom he has corresponded.[26]

You will find the help and advice of dealers to be very important. One of the many delights of book collecting is that of meeting
booksellers. I hardly need to remind you that I am referring to sellers of used books, of whatever vintage. The book dealers are
almost invariably congenial people—a little eccentric, perhaps, but
rarely dull. They seem to be essentially happy people enjoying the
business they have chosen. They are at heart scholars, intellectuals
and book lovers themselves. Most of the time they are on the same
frequency as their customers. Simply tell the bibliophile that you
are a beginner and that you realize you have a lot to learn. He will
probably go out of his way to be of help to you.

It is unlikely that you will ever be swindled by a legitimate bookseller. In many years of dealing with book dealers, both in person
and by mail, with one exception, I have never known anyone to
have been deliberately cheated or deceived. That exception was a
result of my own naïveté. In the sale of my Steinbeck collection for
$24,000, I agreed to pay the dealer six percent commission or
$1,440. Thus I was to receive $22,560. After many weeks, I received
a check for $18,000—a shortfall of $4,560. Also, several years later, I
was examining the letters between the dealer and the library who
had purchased my collection. The actual sale was for $24,500. So I
lost $5,060. However, I had absolutely no recourse or remedy as I
had neither requested nor received anything in writing.

It is embarrassing to admit to such simple-mindedness and to
having been such a trusting fool, but in relating this story, someone else may be spared such an expensive lesson. I hardly need to
add: GET IT IN WRITING.

---

[26]*San Jose Studies*, Vol. 1, No. 3, November 1975.

Even if all parties involved are as honest as Shriners, situations can change and things can happen. People die. They have strokes. Even worse, they get divorces. They go out of business. Acts of God occur. Not to mention acts of Satan. So have adequate insurance for every contingency and get any financial agreement in writing.

Although rare cases such as the deplorable incident just described do occur, any collector can tell stories of the wonderful integrity and conscientious scruples of his or her favorite booksellers. In the early months of my Steinbeck collecting, I found a fine copy of *Bombs Away!* at a famous old San Francisco book shop. I assumed it was a first printing as it was sold as such and in my excitement, I didn't examine it meticulously in the store. After getting it home, while fitting a dust jacket cover on it, I noticed on the back panel, "Second printing." Well, being well acquainted with the principle of caveat emptor, I had the feeling that I had been had. I need not have worried. I took the book back and the gruff but kindly old bookman refunded my money and set out to find me a first printing at the same price. In the following years, I spent hundreds of dollars in that store and urged many other people to shop there.

This story has been told as if it were exceptional, but it is actually routine. Most book dealers operate on the principle that any book may be returned (undamaged and unaltered) without question, within a reasonable time, say, 30 days. If a book is marked "as is" or "w.a.f." (with all faults) then it is sold with the understanding that it is not perfect and that no refund should be expected.

Here is another anecdote that exemplifies the camaraderie and mutual trust that exists in the world of collectible books.

In the lovely old city of Wells in Somerset one blue and white morning in August, I found a book shop just across the lawn from the great cathedral. After becoming lost among the wonderful books for a time, and finally selecting four or five, I noted that I was late for joining the party with which I was traveling. In a frantic hurry, I counted off the pound notes and told the clerk to use the change for postage. I left my card and ran from the store to avoid being stranded. While leaving Wells on the road to Bath, it occurred to me that the dealer could easily keep my money, put the books back on the shelf and I would be absolutely without recourse. About six weeks later, the package arrived at my house some 6,000 miles away, accompanied by a neat

invoice and a vote of thanks. I had not even remembered the
name of the store.[27]

There is about as much cooperation among booksellers as there
is competition, and the competition seems to be of a decent, sporting sort. It is routine for a dealer to refer a customer to a competitor, sometimes even calling the other dealer for the client. Book
people tend to speak well of each other and the entire effect is
reassuring and pleasant for the collector. Exceptions exist, as we
have seen. One of the reasons that the customer seldom witnesses
any bitter rivalry is that there is not that much intense competition over customers. If a dealer can get choice merchandise, he or
she seldom has any difficulty selling it. The real trick in the book
business is acquiring first-rate stock. That is where the real rivalry
is. The key to success in the antiquarian book trade is the skills
and connections that a dealer has in buying. Anyone can sell a
highly prized collector's item to a hyperventilating book maniac.
But few professionals and no amateurs at all can seek out fine
material in top condition and buy it at a price so that it can be re-
sold at a somewhat less than extortionate cost and still turn a
profit. That is where the real competition exists and most customers are unaware of it.

Most dealers are accommodating and helpful insofar as practical but there are occasional exceptions. One collector, for example,
had browsed and bought in a certain bookstore for many years.
He had brought his friends with him many times and had recommended the store to hundreds of people. Then one day, that customer published a book himself and the only thing that the bookseller had to say was to ask how much it cost to have it published—assuming that it had been a "vanity" book. The dealer
would not stock the book or even buy a single copy. And this was
a customer who had spent and caused to have been spent hundreds of dollars in the store. A few bookstores are located on one-
way streets.

On the other hand, another dealer insisted on paying full retail
price for five copies of the customer-author's new book. The old

---

[27]Speaking of dealing with dealers, one of the most delightful books about
books and collecting ever written is by Helene Hanff. It is *84, Charing Cross Road*
(NY: Viking, 1970). "A unique, throat-lumping, side-splitting treasure," *San
Francisco Chronicle*.

man said, "Anyone who does all of the hard work to write a book shouldn't have to give them away or sell them at cost." But this was only typical of that kind man's affectionate and generous character.

Another dealer is notorious for the disconcerting habit of having employees "keep an eye on" browsers. The customer begins to feel like a suspect. You have the right to remain silent...

One of the oldest and best-stocked stores in California had a practice of charging a higher price at the cash register than was penciled into the book itself. The rationale was that the prices had been marked a long time ago and that inflation and appreciation had justified an increase in price. It simply had not been feasible to go through the vast inventory and reprice all of the stock. I bought one of my most prized books in my Mary, Queen of Scots collection there.[28] It was marked $18, a substantial sum for me in 1974. Checking out at the desk, the price was suddenly $38. Sticker shock indeed.

These cases are extraordinary and rarely encountered. It merely indicates that dealers are human like the rest of us and have their bad hair days, too. In most cases, the customer and especially the recognized collector will be accorded the warmest hospitality and accommodation. Some dealers will even allow a bibliophile to take a coveted and expensive book home and pay for it on extended terms. Such trust is to be treasured. If the dealer is expected to be honest, reliable, scrupulous and trusting, then the collector is obliged to be the same. So be sure that your checks are good and pay your bills promptly.

Dealing with dealers by mail can present another dimension to the buyer-seller relationship. A verbal description in a catalog may or may not closely fit the actual condition of a book—what may be "fine" to a dealer may be only "good" to a customer. So there is a certain risk in purchasing by mail. Reputable book merchants will permit return of books within a specified time, and ordinarily, there is no problem.

If I were to make a list of, say, 10 of my all-time favorite books, one of them would surely be *The Cry and the Covenant* by Morton

---

[28]Lionel Cust, *Mary, Queen of Scots* (London: John Murray, 1903). Notes on the authentic portraits. Half calf and marbled boards. First edition. Profusely illustrated. Fine.

Thompson (1949). Reprints and paperback editions seemed to be everywhere but I could not find a fine first in dust jacket. I put an ad in *AB Bookman's Weekly* and in the course of time received a very fine hardback copy in dust jacket. It was not a first edition. The first plainly states on the copyright page. I called the dealer in Ohio (I was in California). He said to send the book and he would return my check, which he did. Not only did the check arrive in a few days but about two months later, I received a very fine first edition of my coveted book. There was no charge for it. Frankly, I think that is being excessively generous, but I was impressed, and I recommended that dealer to everybody I knew.

If you will make your interests known to booksellers, they will be better able to fill your orders. They will know what to look for at auctions and on book-buying excursions. They will know what to buy from book scouts. Sometimes the collector's wants are disarmingly simple. A collector may want to add to his library the first printings of reprint editions. Fine first issues in dust jacket of the books of the Sundial Press, Modern Library, Triangle Books, World, Grosset & Dunlap, etc. are desirable and valuable to many collectors. Fine copies of the Grosset & Dunlap Jack London titles in d.j. find a ready market. A fine first Sundial reprint of *The Long Valley* would probably fetch $40. Tower Books, Large Print Editions, Braille books, International Collectors Library, Heritage Press, etc. are usually beneath the notice of a real Rosenbach[29] but many collectors will snap them up with a minimum of grumbling about the cost. This, by the way, is an interesting phase of bibliophilia which permits the financially limited collector to participate without having to lay out a week's pay for expensive first editions.

It is a good idea to draw up a well-planned "want list" and leave it with your favorite book dealer. Do not leave want lists with more than one dealer at a time. Unpleasant complications can ensue, such as having more than one copy of the same book become available simultaneously. Also, avoid listing items that you cannot afford. You may want a first edition of *Two Years Before the Mast* (NY: Harpers Family Library, 1840) but unless you are ready to pay $4,000 for it, there is no point in entering it on your list.

---

[29]Abraham Solomon Wolfe Rosenbach, dealer, author, collector and scholar. See *Horizon* magazine, November 1960, p. 96.

On the other hand, there is no point in allowing any dealers to drag their feet beyond a reasonable length of time. You may wish to set a limit of, say, three months for him or her to locate some or all of the books on your list. If you do find a book on your list through some other source, by all means, inform the dealer immediately so he or she can call off the dogs.

It is a poor practice to haggle about prices. Normally, the prices listed or quoted by legitimate merchants have been carefully calculated to be competitive and yet sufficiently substantial to keep them in business.

"High-balling" is a selling practice which consists of setting a higher than necessary price on a collectible item—jewelry, furniture, glass, porcelain, books—on the chance of "taking a fish," i.e., finding a buyer with more money than discretion.

"Low-balling" is a selling practice which consists of offering (verbally—never in writing) a lower-than-cost price for the pur-pose of enticing the customer back after he or she has shopped elsewhere. Obviously, this is only done on big-ticket items (several hundred dollars in the case of books) and is risky business. If the shopper comes back after failing to find a comparable item as cheap, the seller must maneuver him or her into an acceptable (to the dealer) price or pretend the item is no longer available.

Although these dubious practices will seldom be found in the antiquarian book trade, they do exist. The Chinese proverb applies when dealing with book dealers, too: "You cheat me once, shame on you; you cheat me twice, shame on me."

Dealers will occasionally offer reduced prices or make discounts to favorite customers. A wonderful old bookseller used to give a generous discount to professors, who, as everyone knows, are scandalously underpaid and cruelly overworked. A few dealers practice lagniappe, i.e., giving the customer an extra book as a bonus. In the country stores of long ago, the merchant would sometimes give the children of a customer a nickel's worth of candy when the old man would buy $50 worth of supplies. That's *lagniappe* (Louisiana French from Spanish *la ñapa* from Quechua *yapa*, "addition"). All of which is to be preferred to haggling. Dealers can be of great service to collectors and this is more likely to happen if you do not become known as a chiseler.

Another advantage of becoming familiar with dealers is that many of them publish catalogs and you can get on their mailing lists. Few publications are more informative or educational to the bibliophile than book catalogs. You should study them even when you have no immediate intention of buying anything. If you have several to consult, you can develop an accurate concept of prevailing prices, relative scarcity and demand. Catalogs are helpful when you are trying to sell your own books. You can determine the value of your books if you find similar copies listed.

It would be of value to you to keep and organize the better class of catalogs that you receive over the years. Some of them are of superb quality and not a few become collector's items themselves. They constitute an excellent reference source for your own collection(s). They are the best means available for determining the rate of appreciation (if any) of books over a period of time. If you paid $25 for a book in 1975 and it now lists for $100, you probably did something right. You can chart that sort of phenomenon by studying catalogs. Allen and Patricia Ahearn describe this aspect of bibliophilia so well, I refer you to their book: *Book Collecting, a Comprehensive Guide,* 1995 edition (NY: G.P. Putnam's Sons, 1995), Pages 5 through 13.

N.B.: When you receive a bookseller's catalog in the mail, drop everything and look to see if there is anything offered in it that is of special interest to you. If so, run (do not walk) to the nearest telephone and call (do not write) immediately to order the desired item. If you delay or if you merely order by mail, the chances are overwhelming that the coveted volume will be sold. You must be aware that you are in competition with many of the other collectors in your field and they get catalogs, too.

Residents of the western United States, Hawaii, and Alaska are at a sharp disadvantage because so many of the great dealers are in the northeastern part of the country. I have known cases where residents of New York received catalogs three weeks before West Coast people received theirs. Arrange to have catalogs air-mailed. It is well worth the minor extra expense.

Let us get back to dealing with the dealer. Never play "one-upmanship" with a veteran dealer. A venerable collector tells us:

Among the folklore of the book collecting business...is
the story of going into the second-hand bookstore and

picking up a book for twenty-five cents that's worth hundreds or thousands of dollars. And that's just what it is: Folklore. It practically never happens. The average dealer knows more about books than any collector; in fact, dealers have wonderful minds. A book collector often collects in one field. He may be a doctor collecting books on medicine, a lawyer collecting books on law...but book dealers know something about books in nearly every field and it always amazes me how much they really do know.[30]

Even so, since the individual collector is often thoroughly erudite in the area of his or her intensely focused interest, occasions arise when the collector may be better informed than the dealer. In fact, the canny bookseller learns from his clients all the time. Bear in mind that the dealer must know hundreds of authors and subjects and the many and varied editions thereof. He or she works at it 40 hours a week, often more. The collector may spend 10 hours a week on the hobby. So the amateur is dealing with the professional. The curators of the special collections at the great university and public libraries are professionals, too. Whereas collectors like us must teach school, cut hair, fight fires, read CAT scans, sell insurance, etc., professionals can spend all of their working time gaining hands-on experience and on-the-job education. And those professionals are all very bright people to begin with. Arguing (not quarreling) with a veteran bookseller is analogous to arguing oncology with your internist. Still, you always have the option of getting a second opinion.

A system that could be used for rating bookstores is based upon the traditional academic grading system: "A, B, C, D." Following are some of the characteristics of bookstores and how I would grade them.

The Grade A store is operated by a true bibliophile with encyclopedic knowledge. He or she must have a willingness to share knowledge in the cooperative and helpful manner of a good teacher. The Grade A store must have a sufficient stock so that one is likely to find something to buy. Neatness and orderliness are nice but not

---

[30]*San Jose Studies,* p. 131. Adrian Goldstone, author of this article, had a wonderful mind himself. Thus his statement is a profound compliment.

required. Convenient parking is a glorious bonus, but not a necessity to qualify. The first-rate bookstore will have an atmosphere of tolerance and respect for the customer. The prospective buyer must be allowed to browse to his or her heart's content with absolutely no obligation to buy anything. But it is a sort of tacit tradition that the customer of an "A" store should buy something, even if it's only a picture postcard or a bookmark. Try to avoid leaving the store empty-handed.

A Grade A dealer will make an effort to cultivate your friendship as well as your custom. He will probably learn your name and greet you by name when you come in again.[31] The wise bibliophile will treat the impoverished book lover as well as his affluent buyers. That emaciated, sandal-shod student may become an orthodontist a few years hence and will remember in color and 3-D which bookseller treated him or her with respect and dignity.

Other symptoms of an "A" establishment (not mandatory) are available catalogs, information about auctions, sales, other dealers, other collectors, etc. Many stores publish catalogs more or less regularly and you can get on their mailing lists usually for the asking.

Some dealers keep extra copies of *Firsts* on hand. This relatively new magazine is published monthly, except July and August when it is bimonthly. It is a superb periodical for the serious collector and has splendid articles of interest to book people. For example, a recent issue had an article on Pulitzer Prize-winning author Wallace Stegner (1909-1993) by Stegner collector and dealer Diane Peterson of Atherton, Calif. To subscribe, address: *Firsts*, P.O. Box 65166, Tucson, AZ 85728.

A thoughtful proprietor will have stools or hassocks for shoppers to rest upon while searching shelves. If shelves are very high, as they are in many stores, there should be ladders. There may be a cup of coffee for the weary book-looker. The absolute, mandatory, required *sine qua non* to qualify as an "A" dealer is an available-to-customers restroom. Nothing—not even book hunting, or

---

[31] About 10 years ago, a lovely Korean lady became the proprietor of a local cleaner. From the first day, she learned and memorized the name of every customer—only the last name—and since then, has greeted each individual entering the place as Mr. Reynolds, Mrs. Gray, Mr. Wykowski, Mrs. Yamashita, etc. It works like magic. People who move across town continue to come back to her cleaners. The same principle, of course, works with any kind of business.

even book finding, is any fun when you are under pressure. Mother Nature, like the medical officer in the army, always has the last word.

The best bookstore in the world is no good to anyone if it's closed. Obviously, students are in school during the day and working people are on the job. The only time they have to shop is in the evening and on weekends. It may not be too wild of a generalization to say that a bookstore would sell more books by being open in the evenings and on weekends than during customary business hours. I realize that everyone who works wants a 9 to 5 job with hourly breaks and three-martini lunches. Even so, it seems that there might be a real opportunity for some bookstores willing to stay open when others are closed.

As you might expect, B, C, and D stores have characteristics in descending order from the standards of the "A" shop. This is not to say that we should avoid the lesser stores. All is forgiven (except an unavailable restroom) if you can find a much-wanted book at a reasonable price. You can park a furlong away, climb hills, mount stairs, push your way through cluttered aisles, endure a surly proprietor and use a flashlight to read by—all with stoic good nature—if you can just find the right book. Fine in dust jacket.

If you want a friend, be a friend. Nearly all bookstores have a supply of business cards on hand. Pick up a few of them and distribute them among your collecting friends and associates. Most stores do not have large advertising budgets; they rely upon word-of-mouth advertising. Many must get by with obscure or inconvenient locations and their business is heavily dependent upon reputation. If the store is good to you and you consider it a good place, a word passed around among your friends can be helpful to the store.

One of the things that you must be meticulous about is prompt payment. If you buy by mail or have an account with a store, be sure to pay your bill with the utmost punctuality. This attention to detail will do much to endear you to the book dealer. I cannot exaggerate the importance of this factor. Pay your bookseller; then pay the rent.

As an English teacher for the past 30 years, I have been a self-ordained missionary for the propagation of reading, for the conversion of students into scholars. I have been willing to try any subterfuge, trick, device or technique to induce my students to read. One assignment has worked well. If you find yourself with unbridled power to invoke such an order, you may find this project effective. For years I have assigned college English students to visit at least two used bookstores. Not new bookstores; we have one of those on campus. Most of the students will be utterly unaware that such businesses even exist and they will find it an interesting experience. They must write a report on their visit and include some tangible evidence (business card, bookmark, photograph) that they were indeed on the premises. I have had countless students tell me—years later in some cases—that one of the best things they learned that year was becoming acquainted with used bookstores.

SELLING YOUR BOOKS

Everyone will at some time find that he has books on hand that he no longer wants. Perhaps they are duplicates resulting from upgrading the collection or just as likely the result of impulse buying. Many books are sold simply because of a shift in the collector's interests. An acute shortage of shelf space can markedly enhance one's culling ability. But from whatever motive, what do you do with the books you want to get rid of?

The quickest and easiest method is to take your books to a legitimate dealer and see if he or she wants them. If so, set your price. As a collector, you must have a fair idea of their value. Set your price. Most dealers dislike being asked, "How much will you give me?" They invariably reply, "How much do you want for them?" anyway. Determine what you think is a fair price and be prepared for a counteroffer. Try more than one dealer if you have the time. The individual characteristics or idiosyncrasies of dealers vary considerably. One may have no use for your books at all; the next may have a customer for just the ones you're trying to sell.

Remember that the dealer must buy at wholesale prices. In the book trade, retail price is about double the wholesale. If you have a book that averages $50 in the catalogs and stores, do not expect the dealer to give you more than about $25 for it. Why should he give you more than he can buy it for from other sources? Unless it is an uncommon book for which he has a waiting customer. In general, I am referring to buying for stock; not buying for a quick turnover. It is much like any other used merchandise business. A car dealer is not going to give you retail for your used car—or your new one, for that matter. Try selling your used camera, computer, binoculars or television set. If you think book dealers tend to be parsimonious in buying books, try a pawnshop sometime. A good rule of thumb in selling books is to consult current catalogs and expect about half of the retail prices listed.

As the value of books go up, the percentage of profit margin may decrease. In the lower price ranges, the dealer must double his money, at least, to stay in business. With inexpensive books, he has to sell a helluva lot of them to make any money. Even if he got a book free, if he sells it for a dollar, he has only made a dollar (less his time and overhead). If he gives $3 for a book, he must get at least $6 to make it worth his time. However, in the loftier ranges of book prices, the situation changes. If the dealer pays $300 for a book and sells it for $400, he can remain financially progressive. A.S.W. Rosenbach of Philadelphia used to say that it was just as easy to sell a $100,000 book as it was to sell a $100 book. It is just as easy to sell a Jaguar as to sell a Geo. Maybe easier.

Just as with an automobile, if you are unwilling to sell at wholesale prices, you can always place an ad in the newspaper or in the *AB Bookman's Weekly.* By referring to book catalogs or Allen and Patricia Ahearn's *Collected Books, the Guide to Values* (NY: Putnam, 1991), you can pretty well determine the value of your books. Figure in the cost of the ad and of your time. Unless you have a substantial number of books of some value, it may not be worth the effort.

There are other possibilities. If you have a friend who has a booth at an antique fair or at a flea market, you may persuade him to allow you to put your books up for sale along with the other merchandise. You may even place them on consignment with a dealer.

You may advertise in bulletins or newsletters published by your employer, school, church, lodge or club. You might pin up "For Sale" cards on bulletin boards. You can almost always get more than wholesale if you have the patience. It all depends on how much of a hurry you're in.

Another point to consider is the donation of your books to a charity store such as Goodwill or the Salvation Army. You might give them to a school library or to a public library. Get a receipt, estimate the value of the books, conservatively, and claim a charitable deduction on your income tax. It could result in an advantage approximating that of selling. Be careful that you can support your claims for any donation. As with any other type of contribution, only fair market value and reasonable claims will be allowed by the Internal Revenue Service.

Don't expect libraries to always want all of your books, and if they accept them, don't expect them to necessarily keep them. I have been librarian for the great Scottish Rite Masonic Temple of San Jose, Calif. for the past 12 years and I know that we receive hundreds of books as donations. Sometimes I can only use a few of those donated, sometimes none at all. Since we do not shelve fiction at all, nor condensed books nor book club editions nor books in any but fine condition, our acceptance rate is at two speeds: Slow and stop. Even so, we can still make use of most books as we can often sell them and put the money in the acquisitions fund.

Some bibliomaniacs are constitutionally and emotionally unable to part with books. They are the Black Holes for books. Books acquired by them go to that far country from whose bourne no traveler returns. In such cases, I might suggest a temporary solution arrived at by collector Robert P. Jackson or Marysville, Calif. He simply converted his two-car garage to a library annex and parked the cars on the driveway. So you don't have to sell. Not just now.

OTHER COLLECTORS

We take care of our health, we lay up our money, we make our roof tight and our clothing sufficient, but who provides wisely that he shall not be wanting in the best property of all—friends.
— Emerson

BOOKSELLERS GENERALLY KNOW the trade thoroughly, especially in their own geographical area, and they can put you in touch with customers of theirs who share your interests. If you are a collector of lexicography, ornithology, ichthyology, Wyoming history, Masonic books or any other kind, your dealer will probably know someone with similar collections. Through mutual interests, friendly relationships of mutual benefit may develop. It is usually both a pleasure and helpful to get to know other specialists in your field. I could recite a world of anecdotes, but I will impose upon your forbearance with only a few.

I was loitering around the shelves and stacks and boxes of books at one of my favorite bookstores one afternoon when the proprietor introduced me to one of the other customers as a "significant collector." He proved to be one of the country's ablest scholars with memberships in the most prestigious bibliophilic societies in the world. His collections included manuscripts (pre-Gutenberg), incunabula, orientalia, association books, letters and memorabilia—altogether a library of some 20,000 volumes. It was my good fortune to have been in the store at that moment. The friendship of such scholars is the best part of an education.

Now this story sounds rather far-fetched but it happened just like this: Some years ago, I was working out in a local gym and conversing with a fellow sufferer. Our talk at the moment concerned my Steinbeck collection and the class that I was teaching at Foothill College featuring Steinbeck's California stories. Another man joined our conversation to ask if I knew George Robinson[32] of Monterey, an old friend of Steinbeck and Ed Ricketts. No, I did not. So Larry Klein (as it was he who had posed the fateful question) provided me with Mr. Robinson's phone number and a proxy introduction. During our telephone conversation, which started another good friendship, Mr. Robinson referred me to "the most knowledgeable teacher of Steinbeck—anywhere." That was Lee Richard Hayman of Salinas High School. Dick had taught Steinbeck in high school and in college for many years in English and in Spanish and had a world-class collection of Steinbeck and of the poet Robinson Jeffers.

Hayman then asked if I were aware that the greatest of all Steinbeck collectors lived in the San Francisco Bay Area. No, I was not aware of that. Mr. Hayman gave me his phone number and that is how my friendship began with Adrian Homer Goldstone, to whom this book is dedicated. Then in the course of several years Robinson, Hayman and Goldstone introduced me to or informed me of other distinguished collectors, scholars and dealers in my special field of interest.

Collectors with common interests can buy, sell and trade among each other. They can share information about sales, dealers, conferences, organizations, publications, courses available, libraries, and yet other collectors. Probably nothing that you will ever do in the course of your book collecting days will prove to be more rewarding than becoming friends with other collectors. The book

---

[32]George Robinson died April 20, 1979. In the early 1930s, he had been personnel director for Del Monte on Cannery Row and had known Steinbeck and Ricketts and all of the characters in Cannery Row and Sweet Thursday. He was also a fine photographer and had many unpublished photographs of historical and literary interest which he donated to the Steinbeck Library in Salinas. He had a wonderful resonant voice and was a superb reader. He made several oral history tapes that can be heard at the Steinbeck Library.

hobby is not an introverted, reclusive activity as it is often stereo-typed. It is as much involved with people as it is with paper.

Collectors with interests different from yours can be valued friends, too. I have found that most bibliophiles are really interest-ed in everything; they are simply compelled by circumstances to specialize in something. Thus you can learn much from collec-tions very different from yours and you can help your friends by keeping an eye out for books of interest to them. They can do the same for you.

In meeting other collectors you will find, especially in the early phases, that they will often have collections that make your own look pitiful and you may begin to feel like an impostor. Never be envious. Do not be discouraged by overwhelmingly greater col-lections. Be patient. You are not the only collector with those inter-ests. Your turn will come. Through persistence, applied hard work and some expense, you can have an enviable collection yourself. Everyone has to start someplace. The great joy is in the collecting, not the collection.

Certainly collectors with differing interests can be good friends, interesting and helpful companions. One friend I remember was a teacher of world history with collections of Eastern history, reli-gion and philosophy. He had an enormous library which he had been working on since he had been a teenager. He knew all sorts of book-finding and money-saving techniques which he cheerful-ly shared with his friends. We had few collecting conflicts of inter-est and I sometimes had the opportunity to be of help to him.

One of the most talented and erudite bibliophiles of my entire experience is a distinguished dermatologist. Besides his obvious interest in medicine, he has what must be one of the greatest col-lections of Darwin and evolution in private hands. In addition, he has impressive collections of Sinclair Lewis, Marjorie Kinnan Rawlings, Winston S. Churchill and World War II. His big house is a veritable library and a museum of horology. He is also a collec-tor of clocks. Since he has so many grateful patients and good friends, they are sometimes able to bring yet another book to add to the wonderful library of the good doctor.

It pays to cultivate friendships with people all over the world. The book trade varies with locality. Some books that are rare in one area may be quite common in another. Try to find an

Australian first edition of *The Moon is Down* in the U.S.A. A U.S. Air Force officer (a former student of mine) found such a book for me at the cost of one dollar in a Sydney bookshop. At the time, none of my fellow Steinbeck collectors had ever seen one.

There is no predicting the source of your next "find." You may pick it up at a garage sale at the square root of its value or you may have to pay more than you had expected. Collectors need to know others who collect books. Your friends, associates, bosses, subordinates, neighbors and relatives can often find books for you if they know what to look for. It is incumbent upon you to make them aware of your interests. One of life's great joys is doing a kindness for others, so don't deprive other people of that opportunity.

Use your own judgment, of course, but consider a well-meant suggestion: Avoid making a profit from your fellow collectors. If you buy a collector's item in the course of your book shopping, sell it to a co-hobbyist for what it cost you. If you have incurred telephone, transportation or postage expenses, it would be reasonable to add those costs, but such favors for friends should involve little or no profit taking. What you do with your books at garage sales, flea markets or with dealers is one thing. What you do with your collector cronies is quite another.

In the event that circumstances are such that you cannot pay a friend immediately when he finds an item for your collection, make a note. Do not ever forget to pay. Your cohort probably will not feel like dunning you for his cost and will end up absorbing the loss. This does not encourage his making finds for you in the future. Even if it is a trifling sum, the principle is the same. Do not be a "slow pay." Slow pay and no pay are both poison.

If you find it impractical to purchase books for henchmen—such as not having sufficient funds at the moment—make a note of the source to inform your colleague of the availability of the books. Do not be too concerned as to whether your friend already has the book you have found for him. If they are collectible editions in fine condition and the price is right, you can always dispose of them. The duplicates you have found may be in better condition than the copies he has so it allows him to upgrade his collection. Or he may be able to trade them to advantage. When in doubt, buy. You will regret not buying a hundred times for every time you will regret making a purchase. Will Rogers once said that he never regretted anything he had done, he just regretted a lot of things he didn't do. Most collectors can testify to the validity of that aphorism.

Make an effort to determine what, specifically, your close fellow-collectors are searching for. Make copies of your own want list and distribute them among book-shopper friends. It is a useful means of extending the range of your hunting grounds.

When you go book shopping, keep the want list of other collectors in mind. It is fun to find a much sought-after and elusive book for a friend. One collector friend, an orthopedic surgeon who specialized in the hand—congenital deformities, diseases, injuries, etc.—had accumulated a library on the hand. One day as I was rummaging through stacks of books at a close-out sale of an old store, I found a fine, bright copy of Kanavel's *Infections of the Hand,* an illustrated first printing of 1914. My friend was delighted to get that great old book and there may be something to the adage that it is somehow better to give than to receive.

There is no present like a book. For birthdays, Bar Mitzvahs, Christmas, anniversaries, graduations...nothing will be received better than the right book for the right person. This applies to almost everybody except the grossly illiterate and it applies especially to the bibliophile.

MISCELLANEOUS SOURCES OF BOOKS

If I have ever made any valuable discoveries, it has been owing more to patient attention than to any other talent.
— Sir Isaac Newton

WHO WOULD COMPARE the discoveries of spectrography, calculus and gravitation with that of used books? Patently absurd, it would seem at first thought. However, the principle may be quite as valid for the one as the other. Even as Newton had to have the genius to deal with the phenomena he "patiently discovered," the hunter of books must have the knowledge and discrimination to identify and evaluate the items he or she finds.

Certainly there is no dearth of used books. They abound. Garage sales, moving-away sales, yard sales, estate sales, library sales, etc. can all be sources for the collector. It is not likely that you will find any first-rate material at such sales, but there is always a chance. That is part of the fun for the bibliophile. You may find a good screwdriver or a repairable toaster, but the likelihood of finding a collectible book varies from slim to none. Householders tend to fall into either of two categories: On the one hand, if they don't know books, they are not apt to have any good ones; on the other hand, if they are biblio-sophisticated, they are not about to part with them at bargain prices. The ideal combination for the book buyer is the householder who has inherited a good accumulation of books and doesn't know anything about them. Not common, but it happens.

A wealthy widow of Los Altos Hills (a suburb of San Jose, Calif.) inherited the books of a great-uncle. She was going to donate them somewhere when a neighbor, suspecting their quality, suggested that she have them appraised. She was very reluctant to pay an appraisal fee and hesitated for a week or so. At last, she relented. As it happened, the first book that the appraiser examined was worth about 10 times as much as his retainer. So if one doesn't know about collectible books, consult someone who does.

A collector of modern first editions told this story: One day he had attended a number of garage sales in several communities, consuming the better part of an otherwise perfectly good Saturday. He thought he would stop at just one more before going home empty-handed and, fortunately for the story, there among the old paint cans and miscellaneous tools, atop a box of snow chains, was a first edition in dust jacket of Faulkner's *Intruder in the Dust* (NY: Random House, 1948). It was priced at $2. In 1972 when this occurred, the book was worth $75. It is now worth $200. We have all heard stories like this—urban legends like alligators in the sewers of New York. Even so, I am convinced that it happens occasionally.

I personally witnessed the following: A former neighbor bought a box of assorted books at an "unclaimed property" auction. She waited until she was home to inspect her purchase and in that box was practically a collection of the books of Edward Gorey.

Sometimes books that are apparently obscure, unimportant and valueless can be very interesting. They can even be quite germane to one's collection. A case history: I collect the books of Barbara Tuchman (Jan. 30, 1912-Feb. 7, 1989). On the occasion of which I write, I had all of her first editions (except her first publication under her maiden name, Wertheim) and was actually looking for first paperback editions and special printings. In the "history" section of a used bookstore in Fresno, I found an old red hardback, *Ambassador Morgenthau's Story* (Garden City: Doubleday Page, 1918), dedicated to Woodrow Wilson. Henry Morgenthau, Sr. (the ambassador to Turkey during World War I) was Barbara Tuchman's grandfather. Her mother was Alma Morgenthau Wertheim. Perhaps of little consequence to most people, it was very interesting to a

Tuchman collector. I later added *Mostly Morgenthaus* by Henry Morgenthau III (NY: Ticknor & Fields, 1991).

Flea markets are rather poor for the serious book collector, but they are better than garage and yard sales. At least there are a lot of books to see. It is something like panning for gold. You have to handle a mountain of gravel to find a nugget. You might enjoy looking for books at flea markets. It is experience in book shopping and appraisal, and if you find a decent item, it won't cost much. Also, flea markets are good places to buy cheap reading copies, paperbacks, etc. as opposed to collector's items.

Paperback or softbound books are cheaply made so that they can be priced at a fraction of the cost of the publisher's hardback editions. For that reason, they are easily damaged and often fall apart after some use. People ordinarily give little attention to their care and maintenance so, in spite of their numerically large printings, fine copies of first paperback printings of important authors are quite scarce. For example, the Popular Library (paperback) edition of Steinbeck's *Cup of Gold* (1949) is quite a minor rarity among collectors and depending on condition, may bring as much as $30. It is common for there to be more than one edition of a paperback title. Collecting the first printings in fine condition is a collecting challenge. The first Dell paperback printing of *The Zimmermann Telegram* was published in 1965, priced at 60 cents. A fine copy of a fragile book 30 years old is not easy to find. I have only seen one copy—the one in my collection. Another paperback of this title was published by Ballantine Books in 1985. Significantly, it was priced at $7.95.

You may wonder why I even mention garage sales and flea markets in a book about the rather sophisticated activity of rare book collecting. It is because first printings of reprint editions, including paperbacks, are usually pretty much ignored by antiquarian bookstores. You are more apt to find Tuchman's *Notes from China* (NY: Collier Books, 1972)—originally priced at $1.25—at a flea market than at an upscale rare book shop. And a real author collection consists of the first printings of all editions, not just the publisher's first editions.

The thorough, meticulous collector will also want the magazines in which the author's stories or articles appeared. In fact, magazine publications are often the very first appearance of such writings. Flea markets can be places where you can find collectible maga-

zines. The *Harper's Magazine* for October 1937, Number 1049 is probably (in fine condition) worth $25. The first appearance of stories by
Steinbeck, Hemingway, Cather, et al. in magazines makes those
publications valuable. Periodicals are not usually stocked at bookstores.

These are generalities that I trust prevail in most cases most of the
time. Collecting all first printings of all editions works fine for an
author who has produced, say, 20 books. But what about Isaac
Asimov and his 200+ titles? You would need an airplane hangar and
the income of a dope dealer. Even collecting the 38 (at the moment)
books of James Michener in all of their permutations would be overwhelming.

So the nature of our collections is governed by their particular
characteristics. With the 11 titles of Barbara Tuchman, an "all-edi-
tions" collection is feasible; with the 60 books of Pearl Buck, it is
daunting.

There is an interesting variable with flea markets. They are not all
the same. They vary from being the outlets of petty thieves to downright fashionable events. There has developed a phenomenon that I
will call the "shopping center sale." This event is called a flea market but it is to the old Parisian type as the affluent suburbs are to the
Latin Quarter. Dealers in jewelry, glass, silver, pewter, brass, dolls,
toys, badges, paperweights, buttons and all sorts of collectibles con-
vene on a shopping mall on weekends and set up shop in front of
the permanent stores. It is a sort of magnified sidewalk sale, the
Ginza of the suburbs. Sometimes you will find a professional bookseller at these shopping center sales—a used bookstore on the side-
walks. You can often find good collectible books at reasonable
prices. But don't go there for bargains. Dealers know too much
about books and their values for you to make any "steals." Bear in
mind that in spite of the bazaar atmosphere and the quasi-flea market environment, you are, for all practical purposes, in a bookseller's
store.

Some other places to practice the art of book culling are the charity or thrift stores. St. Vincent DePaul, Goodwill and Salvation Army
have many well-managed stores with hundreds of books available.
Much of their inventories is made up of book club editions, cheap
reprints, condensed books, old texts, religious propaganda, broken
sets, etc. However, many stores have a lot of good books donated to

them, especially contemporary fiction. Some very collectible authors, e.g., Stephen King, Larry McMurtry and James Michener, are to be found in first trade editions, fine in dust jacket. Most of those books were around $25 new. At the thrift store, they go for seven or eight dollars—or less.

Broken sets can be interesting. Suppose you are collecting, say, Robert Frost. You might find it worthwhile to accumulate the "F" volume of every set of encyclopedias that you find. Most of the articles are different, having been written by different people at different times. The yearbooks that the encyclopedia companies publish can be instructive, too. They report on literary prize awards, publications of established writers, obituaries and other pertinent events. In some cases, collected authors have contributed articles to reference books themselves. Southey's article on Nelson in the eleventh edition of *Encyclopedia Britannica* is one example.

Some sets are designed so that each volume is complete unto itself. The 11-volume *Story of Civilization*[33] is so designed. Individual volumes of William H. Prescott's biographies and histories are scarce and valuable. It seems odd but it often happens: The "biography" volumes in the "collected works" sets, such as those of Irving, Trollope, Dickens, Thackeray, et al. are often preserved while the "works" themselves are abandoned.

One collector, remarkable in the closely focused nature of his collection, had read with great pleasure the works of Sir Walter Scott, especially *Ivanhoe*. He had begun in his youth collecting various editions and printings, especially illustrated editions, of that book. He would sometimes buy whole sets of Scott to get the *Ivanhoe* volume. Then he would give away the rest of the set.[34] His collection ranged

---

[33]Perhaps the most popular work of history ever published, Will Durant's *The Story of Civilization* was published by Simon & Schuster; the first volume, *Our Oriental Heritage*, in 1935 and —Vol. XI, *The Age of Napoleon*, in 1975. Tens of thousands of sets have been sold in the BOMC editions, more yet in Barnes & Noble reprints and the set is now available in the gorgeous leather and gold and moiré edition by the Easton Press. When asked, what is the best book you ever read, I reply: The best book I ever read was in eleven volumes.

[34]I report this story with mixed feelings—admiration for such a remarkable collection and resentment of the ruining of so many sets of Scott. There must be a number of sets around with the *Ivanhoe* volume missing. A broken set is hard to sell and unsatisfactory to own.

from exquisitely bound first editions inscribed by the author all the way to the "Ivanhoe" of the Classic Comics.

Sometimes a valuable collector's item is simply overlooked or is not recognized as such and is put on the shelf in some charity store. After all, the personnel in those stores cannot be expected to be knowledgeable book dealers. In fact, many here in California do not speak English and presumably, do not read the English language in which nearly all the books are printed. In the past decade or so, managers of thrift stores have been engaging the services of book scouts or dealers to go through the book donations. They do that to prevent shoppers from making a book "find" and, of course, to increase their own revenue.

On one occasion at least, I was the beneficiary of a remarkable oversight. One hot summer afternoon, as I was making my usual stop at a particular thrift store, I noted a handsome old green and gold book: *A Yankee in King Arthur's Court.* The copyright page indicated "1889" and on Page 59 there was the "S" before "King" in the caption. A first state of the first edition. A rough estimate of its value: $300 (in 1978). Present value: $450. The price sticker read "89 cents." Needless to say, one "find" like that tends to make one forget all of the futile trips to the thrift stores. It was an extremely rare occurrence, however, and, with current practices, such events are becoming more uncommon all the time.

A word of caution: Avoid becoming known as a bootleg dealer, i.e., a part-time, amateur dealer. The professional bibliophiles who operate their businesses to make a living do not appreciate amateur competition and they won't be apt to do you any favors. Perhaps dealers should be merchants of books, not collectors, and collectors should not be merchants. Ideally, dealers should sell and collectors should buy, and their activities should be complementary, not competitive. However, in practicality, a certain amount of encroachment upon each other's bailiwick is inevitable. Let us strive to minimize it.

A phenomenon that you will probably observe as your collection grows both in quality and in numbers is that you will find fewer and fewer desirable books in thrift stores. The reason, of course, is that at a certain stage in your collection, you will have already found most of the cheap and easy-to-find items for your collection. After that point, the majority of the additions to your library will be obtained from the better class of book stores and from dealer catalogs.

Commercial second-hand merchandise stores often have some books around. They sometimes have bookcases and cabinets around and for the sake of appearance, will have some books displayed in them. The quality is usually about like that of thrift stores, so if you find a collector's item, it is sheer blind luck. However, that is half of the fun of book collecting.

A certain dentist was widely known for his encyclopedic knowledge of dental history. He knew ancient, medieval, Renaissance, Reformation, Enlightenment and Colonial dentistry. He knew more about the Greenwoods' and Paul Revere's and Washington's dentures than you wanted to hear. You would've thought that he had been John Baker's apprentice. At any rate, he was a collector of books on dental history and often made the rounds of bookstores and such places as books are apt to be found. In an antique store one day, the good doctor, after scanning so many rows of books that were incredibly worthless that he was bored, found an old hutch with a shelf of heavy old textbooks. There were two accounting books, a copy of Carl Dunbar's *Geology*, Storer's *Zoology*, a pencil-ruined copy of Maximow and Bloom, and then—a fine bright copy of *Block Anesthesia 1923*, with the name of the collector's former professor on the flyleaf. Not a common book, but not particularly valuable, but for $3, a gratifying and memorable discovery.

A collector of Michener once found a fine first edition of *Death in the Afternoon*. He cordially hated bull-fighting and was not impressed with Hemingway, but he gladly gave $40 for the book knowing it to be worth $200. (It is now worth $1,200.) With the proceeds from that transaction, he bought six fine first editions of Michener. Be alert for good collectible books even if they are not of immediate interest to you.

As a matter of fact, there is a brisk business in what are known as "speculative first editions," especially in the first books of significant authors. Allen and Patricia Ahearn's *Book Collecting, a Comprehensive Guide* (1995) is concerned primarily with authors' first books, their prices and suggestions for collecting. Many quite recent books, such as those of Larry McMurtry and Stephen King are already worth several times their original publisher's prices.

Collecting for speculation is much like any other kind of gam-
bling: It's fun when you're winning. It is another form of collecting perhaps more similar to bookmaking than book collecting.

Auctions can be provocative and productive. Especially if the
operators or owners don't call in the dealers to sandbag all of the
good stuff. Attend some auctions and get the feeling of prevailing
values. Observe the professionals and those of extensive experience. Try a few bids yourself. Occasionally, in sort of desperation,
an auctioneer will knock down a whole box of books for a trifling
sum. On such an occasion, strike like a trout. What do you have to
lose? For a 10- or 20-dollar bill, you may get a box of interesting
or even valuable books. You might get a box of old Watchtower
books, too, and other than effecting the salvation of mankind, you
can't do much with them. They, along with condensed books,
make good insulation.

If you don't want any of your new purchases you can always
donate them to your local thrift store and deduct their value in
itemizing your income tax return. Obtain receipts. It is essential to
avoid arousing the suspicion of the IRS. Your honest deductions
will be allowed and will facilitate your collecting, but don't get
greedy.

A policeman, off duty at the time, was at an estate sale where,
among the furniture, appliances and assorted household goods,
there were several boxes of books. Some of them sold promptly
but a few boxes were left with little interest shown by the onlook-
ers. The auctioneer asked if anyone would give five dollars and
the officer found himself the owner of a box of books. He began
digging into the contents and there were the usual old textbooks,
Bibles, condensed books and reprints of old novels. On the bottom was a fine bright copy of Frost's *New Hampshire*, a first edition of 1923. No dust jacket but still, a nice collector's item. How it
ended up in a box of worthless books at a small town sale is
another of the mysteries of bibliophilia.

Another miscellaneous source: Besides library sales, second-
hand stores, thrift stores, etc. one of the more obvious sources of
used books is the want-ad section of your local newspaper. Many
families have had books on hand for years and for a variety of
reasons have simply kept them because they did not know what
to do with them. Occasionally, they will advertise to sell them.

Ordinarily, such books can be bought at reasonable prices. A colleague once bought a fine set of the eleventh edition of the *Encyclopedia Britannica* in limp leather on india paper through such an ad. The set was in the original mahogany cabinet that had been designed for it. Her cost was about a third of the appraised value later determined.

You might advertise as a buyer. Suppose that you are interested in collecting the works of William Manchester. Place an ad in the local paper. The cost is trifling and you may be astonished to learn how many people have books on hand that you want. They are as anxious to sell as you are to buy.

Of all the sources of inexpensive books, the best is the "Friends of the Library" book sale. It is also one of the most common sources of acquiring stock for your local used bookstore. The "Friends of the Library" idea works like this: The library solicits donations of books from local citizens. The people donate books to the library. The library gets the books for nothing and the donor gets his tax deduction. The library then conducts a sale to the general public, pricing books very attractively. The public gets to buy books at low cost and the library gets the money with which to buy new books. It is a splendidly simple system that works beautifully.

This is the best thing you can do to build your personal library. Go to every public library within range and learn the dates and times of their sales. Go in person and buy a membership in their "Friends of the Library" program. The sum is negligible and it, too, will go toward new acquisitions. Attend every sale you can. Be there on time. Bring a box to hold your selections, as you cannot conveniently carry books in your arms and browse at the same time. There is nothing wrong with buying books at these sales for resale. That's what the dealers do. And you can get to be as fast at book grabbing as they are. Study booksellers' catalogs and Ahearn's *Collected Books, the Guide to Values.* Buy collectible volumes and sort them out later. Keep the ones you want and dispose of the rest at your leisure. When in doubt, buy. You can always get the paltry sum you paid for any book at a "Friends" sale, and even if you can't, you can donate it to your favorite thrift store.

Usually the Friends of the Library organization limits the first day or evening of the sale to members only, which is reason enough for joining.

Some colleges have what amounts to a "Friends" sale. DeAnza College of Cupertino, Calif. regularly sets aside Wednesday mornings for a sale of discards, ex-libs and donated books.

Bring all the cash you can afford. Small bills and change can be of help and convenience to the library personnel. Many are reluctant to accept checks and they do not usually have facilities to use credit cards. The attendants at these sales are volunteer workers who serve without pay so any cooperation you can give them will be appreciated.

Other sales of this nature are held by various non-profit groups —fraternal orders, lodges, disease support groups, etc. Churches conduct bazaars and rummage sales and there are usually some books. The quality varies from dismal to fair but possibilities exist and the prices are right.

Conducting book sales is only one function of the Friends of the Library. They handle publicity for the library and sponsor lectures. Most chapters have several standing committees at any given time and they can often use your help. Donating your time and working with the Friends can be a rewarding experience and an education for any book lover.

When you buy used books, especially those that seem to have been stored in boxes for some time, let me suggest that you hold each of the books vertically, spine up and riffle the pages. Many old books have interesting material stashed between the pages. This is called "hay" in the trade. You never know what will come fluttering out of some old book.

An antiques dealer once bought a fine Grabhorn book in a slipcase and later showed it to a friend. Her friend asked playfully, "Can I keep anything I find in this book?" About midway between the 300 pages were two 20-dollar bills.

AN ESSAY ON BOOKS

AS DELIGHTFUL AS books can be, they are not necessarily always good things. Books may be misleading, distorted, honestly mistaken, meretricious, or evil. *Mein Kampf* is virtually all of those things and is as evil as its author. *Das Kapital* was sincerely presented to the world by a well-meaning scholar, but he was mistaken. *Millions Now Living Will Never Die* (a Watchtower publication) is merely foolish.

Religions are often founded on illusions and perpetuated by lies and deception. Hence the "holy" books which apotheosize myth, legend and nonsense acquire a patina of infallibility that is patently fatuous. Much worse than fatuous, such books often inspire vicious atrocities such as crusades, jihads and pogroms. And, as Luther wisely observed, as he urged the massacre of the peasants: "The Devil can quote Scripture to suit his purpose."

Now consider the millions of man-hours expended over the many centuries since the Babylonian star-gazers contrived their Rorschach images in the zodiac. Aries and Cancer and Gemini and Virgo indeed! What might mankind have accomplished if he had devoted all of that time and energy and intelligence to the study of true things? Even so, nothing is ALL bad. Not even astrology.[35] It eventually fathered the true science of astronomy.

How many people have gone to premature graves (many of them children) because of a book that teaches that its special form of prayer is more effective in the cure of disease or injury than vaccines, antibiotics, insulin and surgery? How many otherwise innocent people have suffered needlessly for years when medical remedies were easily available?[36]

What a work is man, who creates gods by the thousands and who cannot even make a worm. Faith healers can cure multitudes of the most hideous of diseases yet cannot even restore a simple amputation or a missing tooth.

Fiction is not necessarily untrue and non-fiction is not always true, even when sincerely intended to be. Masterpieces of fiction may be true in allegory or metaphor while almost disregarding factual data. Shakespeare's "Macbeth" takes liberties with the history of Scotland, but as a drama of human nature, it is an eternal treasure. On the other hand, much of the pioneering work of Fracastoro, Vesalius, Servetus, et al. has been either invalidated or superseded. Humoral pathology, once de rigeur in medicine, is now merely a historical relic.

In collecting a subject—medicine, physics, Freemasonry, astronomy, the Jesuits, architecture, etc.—it is not fair to collect only those books or authors which support your own beliefs or preferences. In a parody of physics: For every idea or theory there is an equal and opposite idea or theory. So if you collect books about the Mormons, you should collect books that praise and defend the L.D.S. as well as debunk them.

If a person can be known by the company he keeps, he could also be known by the books he owns.[37] No matter at what age, we

---

[35]For a thorough humiliation of astrology, read "Unlucky Stars for Astrologer—UC Scientist Test Claims," *San Francisco Chronicle*, Thursday Dec. 5, 1985, p. 8.

[36]Faith healing has been debunked over and over for many years but seems itself to be incurable. For a recent discrediting, see James Randi, *The Faith Healers* (Buffalo: Prometheus Books, 1987) with a brilliant foreword by Carl Sagan. Sherwin B. Nuland, M.D., has written very well about "healing" frauds in several books.

[37]"All good books have one thing in common—they are truer than if they had really happened, and after you have read one of them you will feel that all that happened, happened to you and then it belongs to you forever."—Ernest Hemingway

are going to be bored and lonely during much of our lives. Readers are seldom bored or lonely. They can communicate with, learn from and be entertained by any of hundreds of the best minds that have lived over the many centuries. The person who taught you to read was the greatest benefactor you ever had.

LES NOMMES DE PLUME

What is in a name? That which we call a rose, by any other name would smell as sweet.

— Shakespeare

NICKNAMES, PEN NAMES, aliases, incomplete names and the use of mere initials (A.E., H.D., e.g.) are all commonly found throughout history. Yahweh changed Jacob's name to Israel. The name of Yahweh himself was never uttered by his pious children and a number of substitutes for the Ineffable Name was found. Yahweh or Jehovah were merely later crude attempts to pronounce the Hebrew letters which we transliterate as JHVH, YHVH, JHWH or YHWH. In fact, nearly all of the original names in the Bible are markedly different when mispronounced in modern European languages, especially Jacobean English.

Amenhotep IV, Pharaoh from 1375 to 1358 B.C., changed his own name to Ikhnaton in his role as religious reformer. Plato (Greek Platon, "flat"—modern cognate, "plateau") was the nickname of Aristocles who died in 347 B.C. Marcus Tullius Cicero (101-43 B.C.) is known to us simply as Cicero, and who remembers that Virgil was Publius Vergilius Maro? St. Paul of the Epistles had been Saul of Tarsus and Caesar Augustus had been Octavian.

The Latin word alias means "otherwise" (known as) and has been in use since ancient Roman times. For centuries, men and women have been discarding their family names as they entered orders, convents and monasteries. Cardinals changed their names when becoming popes. The only Englishman to ever become a pope, Nicholas Breakspear, became Adrian IV from 1154 to 1159. Alexander VI (Pope 1492-1503) was Rodrigo Borgia. The Borgias had come from Spain, where their name had been Borja. Guilio Mazarine became a naturalized citizen of France and is known to history as Jules Cardinal Mazarin (1602-1661).

Many of the great names from medieval and Renaissance times, as the names are popularly known, are either incomplete or aliases. Most commonly, artists and writers are known to us by their first or baptismal names. Giotto diBondone is practically never known by his full name. Neither is Dante Alighieri, Raphael Sanzio or Michaelangelo Buonarotti. Sometimes writers are known by their family names. This is the case with Francesco Petrarco (Petrarch) and Torquato Tasso.

Tiziano Vicelli, alias Titian (1477-1576) is rarely known by his family name. Geert Geerts is more familiar as Erasmus. Tintoretto was baptized Jacopo Robusti. Kyriakos Theotokopoulos was simply called "The Greek" in Spain where he lived and painted. Hence he is known as El Greco (1548-1614).

It was once popular for distinguished persons to Hellenize or Latinize their names, sometimes with dramatic effect. Philip Schwarzerd, Luther's disciple, translated Schwarzerd ("Black Earth") to the Greek equivalent, Melanchthon. The pioneer physician Theophrastus Bombastus Von Hohenheim (1493-1541) became Paracelsus (i.e., "Greater than Celsus"). Miguel de Serveto Latinized his name to Servetus (1511-1553). Andre Wesal, the Flemish anatomist (1514-1564) is known to fame as Vesalius.

Another source of confusion is the phenomenon of titles of royalty or nobility. Elizabeth's Leicester would not be recognized by most readers as Robert Dudley. Henry Tudor ("Tudor" is Cymric for "Theodore," which is Greek for "gift of God") became the Duke of Richmond before he was Henry VII. Queen Anne's military genius, Marlborough, was John Churchill. Sometimes the family name is better known than the title. This is the case with the Earl of Beaconsfield, who is better known as Benjamin Disraeli (originally D'Israel).

Pseudonyms are found in all varieties and conditions of folk in our life's journey. Trotsky was Lev Bronstein. Stalin (Russian for "steel" which word was borrowed from German Stahl) is a nickname for the Georgian peasant Iosif Vissarionovich Dzhugashvili. Tito was once Josip Broz. Vladimir Ilich Ulyanov (1870-1924) is not immediately familiar to most people, but as the first premier of the Soviet Union, his pseudonym is universally infamous.

Many names, particularly those of show-business people, are changed for sheer euphony, i.e., someone thinks the new name sounds better. So Leonard Slye becomes Roy Rogers. Doris Kapelhoff becomes Doris Day, and Nathan Birnbaum somehow doesn't appeal to the ear as well as George Burns. And surely Marion Morrison would never have been the heroic figure that John Wayne was. Pronunciation difficulties motivate many name changes. It is easier for English-speaking people to say Maria Callas than it is to say Cecilia S.S.M. Kalogeropoulos. Issur Danielovich became Izzy Dimsky but even that was not as easy for Americans to pronounce as Kirk Douglas.

Anti-Semitism, especially in earlier generations, was a powerful reason for name changes among Jewish people. It is conceivable that Emmanuel Goldenberg may not have been able to get into show business, or if so, the struggle would've been much tougher than it was for Edward G. Robinson. Would Eddie Cantor have made it if he had remained Izzie Itzkowitz? Would Bernie Schwartz have made all of those movies that made Tony Curtis rich and famous? Further examples could be cited by the dozen, from Al Jolson to Jerry Lewis. But times they are a-changing. Now David Wallechinsky can publish *The Book of Lists* with his father, Irving Wallace. Aaron Spelling and Steven Speilberg make no attempt to conceal their Yiddish names. Why should they?

There used to be a persistent bias against women in the arts in general and literature in particular—and not so long ago. Although there were a few female writes here and there around the world, such as Sappho and Lady Murasaki, in Europe there were virtually none until late in the 18th century. Some published as "Mrs. _____" as with Mrs. Haskell and a few used single names, such as "Ouida." Although Jane Austen published under an obviously feminine name, she was exceptional. Even the great Brontë sisters first published under ambiguous masculine-appearing names. George Eliot was really Mary Anne Evans. George Sand also felt that she had to write as a man in order to be accepted and read. Even recently, who would guess, if he did not know, that Carson McCullers, Harper Lee, Taylor Caldwell, and P.D. James were women? Certainly the names do not suggest femininity. Gender biases have subsided in recent decades, but even so, until Toni Morrison was nominated last year, Pearl Buck (1938) was the only American woman to ever win the Nobel Prize for literature.

Since there is such a plethora of excellent writers in our modern electronic world with its computers and word processors, its satellite communications providing instantaneous television throughout the world, perhaps the Nobel Prize for literature could be decentralized or "de-focused." Suppose there were a Nobel Prize for fiction and one for non-fiction? Then superb historical and biographical writers such as William Manchester would not compete with fiction writers such as John Irving.

It might be legitimate to suggest that instead of bestowing an $800,000 fortune on a single recipient, we should award eight prizes of $100,000. There might be a prize for, let's say, science fiction, crime-murder mystery (detective), war novels, love stories, horror-suspense books and whatever others an erudite committee might select. Although the Nobel Prize is a world-class award made for the life's work of an author, the suggestion could still have some validity. Many fine writers are pretty well type-cast in certain genres. In fact, some writers even resort to publishing under another name, i.e., under a name different than the one made famous in a particular genre.

For whatever reason a writer sought to become known under a name (sometimes several names) other than his or her own, it may prove useful to have some kind of manageable guide to pseudonyms.[38]

---

[38]For a general idea of the vast extent of this subject, see *Anonyma and Pseudonyma* (Stonehill, Block & Stonehill, London, 1926), 4 vol., 3,447 pp. Also c.f. William Cushing, *Initials & Pseudonyms, a Dictionary of Literary Disguises* (NY: Crowell, 1885), 603 pp. Also Allen and Patricia Ahearn's fine *Collected Books, the Guide to Values* (1991).

Most books about books, such as this one, are hopelessly inadequate and unequal to the job of listing enough names and pseudonyms to be comprehensive. There are just too many. In studying the phenomenon, one gets the impression that it is, indeed, the exceptional author who first publishes under the name that appeared on his or her birth certificate and who kept the same name during his or her entire career.

Collecting mystery fiction and science fiction is often confusing and frustrating because writers of such books are frequently very prolific. They are sometimes so prolific that they tend to wear out their welcome. To avoid sales resistance, they simply publish under another name.

Suppose you are collecting the early books of Albert Gunzel and suddenly in a given year, no more books are to be found under that name. Then the same year that Gunzel quit publishing, books of a similar style begin appearing under the name of Ernest Bugtussel. Thus many collections require sorting out of various names as employed by writers at different periods during their careers.

It is always desirable for the bibliophile to have a bibliography or at least a checklist for the collection on which he or she is working. Those convenient reference books will indicate the other names (if any) that your author used and which titles match which names. If no check lists or bibliographies are available, consult the indexes of books about books and authors. If research problems remain unresolved, consult the research librarian at your public library or your ABAA bookseller. Such a problem may seem unlikely, but with extremely prolific authors, it is not so remote. Try collecting John Creasy.

When you consider that Georges Simenon alone has written 220 novels under his own name and 150 under various pseudonyms, it makes you want to change the subject. For another spectacular example of the lavish use of literary disguises, the following names have all been used by a single writer, John Creasy:

Gordon Ashe	Patrick Gill
M.E. Cooke	Michael Halliday
Normal Deane	Charles Hogarth
Robert Caine Frazer	Brian Hope

Then to add to the confusion, there is the case of one pen name being used by more than one writer. Frederick Dannay and Manfred Lee both used the name Ellery Queen. They also wrote under the name Barnaby Ross.

It is virtually impossible to exaggerate the incredible complexity of the subject of pseudonyma, not to mention anonyma, that is, anonymous. Sir Walter Scott published *Waverly* anonymously and his following novels were published by "The Author of Waverly." Sometimes, for bibliographic and book collecting purposes, it is helpful to know about literary aliases. The following is a pitifully brief list of some of the better known pen names with matching "real" names.

Pseudonym	*Real Name*
A.E.	George Russell
Owen Aherne	R.V. Cassill
Anthony Abbott	Fulton Oursler
Richard Bachman	Stephen King
Frank Baker	Sir Richard Burton (the 19th century Burton)
Acton Bell	Anne Brontë
Currer Bell	Charlotte Brontë
Ellis Bell	Emily Brontë
Josh Billings	Henry W. Shaw
Edgar Box	Gore Vidal
Boz	Charles Dickens
Max Brand	Frederick Faust
Tom Brown	Thomas Hughes
Tex Burns	Louis L'Amour
Nick Carter (also Jake Logan, Martin Quinn, Simon Quinn)	Martin Cruz Smith
Lewis Carroll	Charles L. Dodgson
Agatha Christie	Agatha M.C. Mallowan
Paul Connally	Tom Wicker
Joseph Conrad	Teodor Josef Konrad Nalecz Korzeniowsky
Marie Corelli	Mary Mackay
Philippa Carr, Victoria Holt, Jean Plaidy, Elbur Ford, Eleanor Burford, Kathleen Kellow, Ellalice Tate	Eleanor Burford Hibbert
Clemence Dane	Winifred Ashton

Frederick Douglass	Frederick Augustus Washington Bailey
Elia	Charles Lamb
George Eliot	Mary Ann Evans
Mark Epernay	John Kenneth Galbraith
A.A. Fair, Charleton Kendrake, Charles J. Kenney	Erle Stanley Gardner
Anne Fairbairn	Dorothy Tait
Ford Madox Ford	Ford Madox Hueffer
Webster Ford	Edgar Lee Masters
Gene Fowler	Gene Devlan
Anatole France	Anatole Thibault
Cynthia Freeman	Bea Feinberg
Paul French, Dr. A	Isaac Asimov
Maxim Gorky	A. Max Peshkov
Tom Graham	Sinclair Lewis
H.D.	Hilda Doolittle
O. Henry	Sidney Porter
Jack Higgins, Martin Fallon, Hugh Marlowe, James Graham	Harry Patterson
Jeffrey Hudson, John Lange	Michael Crichton, M.D.
Michael Innes	John Innes Mackintosh Stewart
Benjamin F. Johnson	James Whitcomb Riley
John LeCarré	David Cornwall
Andrew Lee	Louis Auchincloss
John Macdonald, Ross Macdonald, John Ross Macdonald	Kenneth Millar
Andre Maurois	Emile Herzog
Owen Meredith	First Earl of Lytton (son of Sir Edward Bulwer-Lytton)
Molière	Jean Baptiste Poquelin
Charles Norden	Lawrence Durrell
George Orwell	Eric Blair
John Leslie Palmer	Hillary Aiden St. George Saunders
Phiz (Dickens' illustrator)	Hablot K. Browne
Mary Renault	Mary Challans
John Rhode	Cecil Charles John Street
Sax Rohmer	Arthur S. Ward
George Sand	Amandine Lucile Aurore Dudevant, *nee* Dupin
John Sedges	Pearl S. Buck
Saki	Hector Hugh Munro
Poor Richard (Saunders)	Benjamin Franklin

Dr. Seuss	Theodore Seuss Geisel
Johnston Smith	Stephen Crane
Stendahl	Marie Henri Beyle
Henry Sutton	David Slavitt
Studs Terkel	Jerome Terkel
Josephine Tey	Elizabeth Mackintosh
Michael Angelo Titmarsh	William Makepeace Thackeray
Mark Twain	Samuel Langhorne Clemens
S.S. Van Dine	Willard Huntington Wright
Voltaire	François Marie Arouet
Irving Wallace	Irving Wallechinsky
Artemus Ward	Charles Farrer Browne
Rebecca West	Cecily Isabel Fairfield Andrews
Edith Wharton	Edith Newbold Jones

Perhaps "pseudonym" is a poorly chosen word for the phenomenon of name change. The Greek root "pseud" means "false," as in the amoeba's pseudopod or in such compounds as "pseudo-scientific." In the literary context, no aspersions upon the author's character or honesty are implied by the use of the term. The word includes the use of married names, maiden names, initials (A.E.), nicknames (Boz) or made-up names (Mark Twain). No comparison to Dutch Schultz (Arthur Flegenheimer) or Waxey Gordon (Gordon Wechsler) or other denizens of the underworld is intended.

PHOTOGRAPHY AND THE BOOK COLLECTOR

THE FIRST BOOK illustrated with photographs was *The Pencil of Nature* by Henry Fox Talbot in 1843. Since then photographs have become increasingly more commonplace and useful. Matthew Brady caused the U.S. Civil War to be the first photographed war,[39] as a century later the Vietnamese War was to be the first televised war.

Many books are so beautifully and appropriately illustrated with photographs that the text almost seems secondary. Such is the case with Steinbeck's *The Forgotten Village* (Viking, 1941), illustrated with movie stills, and *A Russian Journal* (Viking, 1948). *Steinbeck Country* by Steve Crouch (Palo Alto: American West, 1973) is strikingly beautiful. The text is superb and is in many passages reminiscent of Steinbeck himself, but it is clearly subordinate to the masterful photography. Thus photography has developed to such a fine art that it rivals the texts of many books.

---

[39]There were photographs taken in the Crimean War about 10 years before the U.S. Civil War, but there were not many and were never much publicized.

Steinbeck's *America and Americans* (Viking, 1966) is primarily photographic. The text is little more than picture captions.

The role of photography in modern book production can hardly
be exaggerated, but photography is like oxygen. It combines well
with almost anything. It works well in combination with book
collecting and if you are not already interested in taking pictures,
you may well consider merging that art with your bibliophilia.

The world is full of literary landmarks. Take a good camera
with you on your travels and you can add a whole new dimension to your library. Suppose you collect Hemingway. His birthplace is in Oak Park, Ill. His boyhood haunts where he and his
father, Clarence Hemingway, M.D., hunted and fished, are in
upper Michigan. There is a monument to the writer at Cojimar on
the coast of Cuba where Castro's government still keeps
Hemingway's old fishing boat, the Pilar, in museum condition.
Cojimar is the place where Hemingway was inspired to write *The
Old Man and the Sea.*[40] Besides his estate at Finca Vigía near
Havana, Hemingway had a beautiful home (now a tourist attrac-
tion) in Key West, Fla. There is a statue of Don Ernesto in
Pamploma where he and his friends once romped with the bulls.
In Paris there is the Gertrude Stein house where he and F. Scott
Fitzgerald and Ford Madox Ford and others made themselves
familiar. He lies buried with an evergreen at either side of his simple marble slab in a little country cemetery near Ketchum, Idaho.
In August of 1967, I photographed the grave site with the two little trees which had been there for only six years. It was a lovely
picture with the great hill in the background and beyond the hill,
sapphire-blue sky and cotton-ball clouds. Many years later, Dr.
Medford of Marysville, Calif. sent me a picture he had taken of
the same site with the trees now some 10 or 12 feet tall. A trivial
thing, perhaps, but to people who loved Hemingway and his
wonderful stories, such an experience has a nostalgic quality and
a kind of serenity that is rare and precious to the heart. Rest in
peace, Don Ernesto, far from the madding crowd, under the skies
of one of the loveliest places on earth.

Thus there can be much more to book collecting than the mere
acquiring and arranging of books. And now with video cameras,

---

[40] See "He Fights for Hemingway," by Larry Smith, *Parade* magazine, July 2,
1995.

an even greater sophistication of photography is possible. Not merely possible, but easy and convenient.

You can work out reciprocal arrangements with other collector-photographers. If you happen to be in Mississippi in the Faulkner Country around Oxford, you might get some pictures for a Faulkner collector. In Atlanta, photograph the Joel Chandler Harris home. In North Carolina, you would find places of interest to O. Henry and Thomas Wolfe collectors. New York and New England are too rich with literary associations to mention. Boston alone would be a major project in literary landmarks.

For several years, an academic colleague and I exchanged photographic favors. He was a scholar of the Church of Jesus Christ of Latter Day Saints, collected Mormoniana, visited great collections of Mormon material, visited and photographed the fabulous Mormon temples. Most of the temples are magnificent but some are absolutely awesome (e.g., Oakland, Calif. and Washington, D.C.). I took pictures of Mormon temples in the course of my travels and sometimes, they were of temples that my colleague had not been able to visit.

I was librarian of the San Jose, Calif. Scottish Rite Masonic Temple and made it a practice of visiting Scottish Rite temples wherever my travels took me. Of course, I couldn't possibly see them all so my Mormon friend supplemented my collection in the course of his travels.

The practice of collecting material relating to the author and to the places he wrote about is a very old one. You can, like Dante (1265-1321) visit the grave of Virgil (70-19 B.C.) when you are in Naples. Photograph the grave of Keats in the Protestant Cemetery in Rome. It was already a mecca for English and American visitors when Charles Eliot Norton tidied it up in the 1850s.

There are entire books concerned with authors and the locales of their lives and their works. England is particularly rich in literary associations and references and such books as *About England with Dickens* by Alfred Rimmer or *Literary Landmarks of London* by Laurence Hutton are typical of older books of this nature. William Dean Howells wrote at least two good books of the literary travel genre. For a modern book of this nature, see *The Oxford Literary Guide to the British Isles* (Oxford: The Clarendon Press, 1977).

Travel guides and travel books, ancient, old, recent and new
abound in great numbers.

You can make a collection of photographs of your own literary
landmarks and integrate them with your books. Since you would
be collecting, presumably, only one author or subject, it might
well be a feasible project to do your own landmark photographs.
If you are collecting the works of a living author, you may get pictures along with autographs and inscriptions.

For 10 years, I collected the works of Pulitzer Prize (1972)
author Wallace Stegner. Since he lived less than 10 miles from my
house, I often visited with him and of course, had him inscribe all
of the books. In the course of this unique experience, I took many
photographs.

One June day in 1975, I went with Steinbeck scholar-collectors
Adrian Goldstone and Norman Carlson to visit Nelson Valjean.
Mr. Valjean lived not far from Goldstone's house in Mill Valley,
Calif. He had just published his book, *John Steinbeck, Errant Knight*
(San Francisco: Chronicle Books, 1975), an intimate and profusely
illustrated (photographs) biography. Valjean and Steinbeck had
been roommates at Stanford and friends later for decades. I took
many pictures that day, of the author and of my distinguished
companions. It was fortunate that I did because only three
months later, Valjean was dead. On that June day, Goldstone had
exactly two years to live. Those pictures, association items of the
Steinbeck collection, are unique and eventually became part of the
archives of a major Steinbeck collection.

George A. Robinson (mentioned earlier in this book) was a fine
professional photographer who lived for many years in a hillside
home overlooking Monterey's Cannery Row. Many of the routine
photographs that Robinson made during the 1930s and 1940s are
now museum pieces. They are of great interest as they caught the
mood and tone of the time and of the places Steinbeck made
famous in his Monterey tales.

Mr. Robinson died on April 20, 1979 and his ashes were scattered over his beloved Monterey Bay. He was an artist—and photography is a fine art—and a cheerful, likable companion. He was
not a collector himself. He was not very good at keeping things.
His pleasure was in giving things away and the collections of his
friends are richer for his art and his generosity.

If you choose not to do your own photography with your collecting, you can usually buy pictures, prints, postcards, etc. in the area of your interest. For example, Steinbeck's home and birthplace at 132 Central Ave. in Salinas has been converted to a gourmet restaurant and the basement is a boutique called "The Best Cellar." All sorts of memorabilia are available, most of it very interesting to collectors of Steinbeck's works.

The Burns and Scott country of the lowlands of Scotland has a veritable industry in souvenirs of the poets. It would be more gratifying to do your own photography, but sometimes it is not possible. Sometimes it is not permitted. So souvenirs, art work, prints, posters, postcards and other ephemera may enrich and expand the quality of your collection.

If you belong to a literary association, such as a library associates group or an author society, your photographs of members, guest speakers, etc. could be of great interest, perhaps eventually comprising a pictorial history of the organization.

Another factor is worth considering. If you ever have occasion to write a thesis, article or book on your subject, your photographs could be of tremendous value to you.

Always err in the direction of taking too many pictures. You can always cull out and discard poor pictures or duplicates. You can rarely get the same people or the same scene together again. Use the best camera, accessories and film that you can possibly afford. Do not skimp on the expense of developing film. If you do not do your own developing, get the best service available. Quality is remembered long after price is forgotten—especially in photography.

SOUND RECORDING

The sound must seem an echo to the sense.
— Alexander Pope

IT MAY SEEM strange to find a chapter on sound recording in a book about book collecting. However, oral history, i.e., material committed to sound recordings instead of print, has become increasingly popular. For example, the Steinbeck Library of Salinas, Calif. has nearly a hundred hours of recordings. The material includes readings by Steinbeck himself, local history interviews with people who had known the family and with personal friends of the author. George Robinson was an eloquent storyteller with a particularly resonant and charming voice. The recordings that he made are now prized possessions of the library.

Many of the suggestions about photography apply to the art and science of sound recording. With the fine compact equipment available, with simple controls and operating procedures, anyone should find it easy to make good quality recordings.

With the ubiquitous video camera, VCR, TV monitor and new digital technology, conventional photography and tape recording may become increasingly obsolescent. Even so, you can't replace the book for the true bibliophile.

As a book collector-scholar-adventurer-traveler, you may wish to avail yourself of state-of-the-art information accessing and storage. You may want a record of a lecture or even of a conversation with a person important to your subject. If you do any teaching or lecturing yourself, recordings can add an excellent feature to your presentations. Among the more obvious possibilities is the use of recordings of radio broadcasts relevant to your collection. With the efficient light-weight equipment now available, it would be no herculean effort for a collector to assemble a video collection of great interest. TV tapes of the movies that have been made from the works of your author would be a fairly simple matter.

Dr. Audrey Lynch[41] often gives presentations on Steinbeck to schools, libraries and literary groups and makes effective use of sound and graphics.

When you photograph or record, get the permission of those involved. Ordinarily it is a mere formality, as perfunctory as a greeting. But if for any reason the lecturer or guest of honor declines permission, put your equipment away. It is no more than common courtesy. The material covered by the speaker may be part of a book or article he is writing and he may be reluctant to have it recorded. There may be complications of copyright.

Some public figures such as authors are actually quite shy. While expansive and creative in their private world, they may be uncomfortable and inhibited in public, particularly when their every word is being recorded. Be considerate of their feelings. When taking pictures and making recordings, be as unobtrusive as a shadow. Cast a low profile and be as quiet as an old grave-yard ghost. It is sufficient that you have been given permission to make records. The least you can do is to avoid disturbing the audience and participants. Your recording is a privilege, not a right.

---

[41]Author, with Sparky Enea, of *With Steinbeck in the Sea of Cortez* (Los Osos, CA: Sand River Press, 1991).

SPECIAL GUEST CHAPTER

BOOK COLLECTING—THE HOBBY THAT CHANGED MY LIFE

By MICHAEL QUIGLEY, M.D., Ph.D.

A Vietnam War amputee and former prisoner-of-war, the late Dr. Michael Quigley, an epidemiologist by training, was a leading collector of Stephen Crane, Carl Sandburg and James A. Michener. He wrote this chapter shortly before his death in October 1996. His lifelong love of books was transformed into a passionate love affair and a new second career to a large degree by meeting the author on a Holland America cruise ship in 1982. Dr. Quigley spent more than 20 weeks each year traveling, mostly as a consultant, lecturer and rare book collector on major cruise ships throughout the world, only occasionally serving in the capacity of ship's doctor. He donated a lot of time to disabled veterans and was a leading advocate for them and his fellow disabled people the world over. When not cruising and book collecting, he spent time at his book-filled home on a large ranch in East Texas with his constant companions, Lord Wellington and Sheba, Silkie Terriers from New Zealand and Australia, respectively.

WHILE I'VE ALWAYS been very interested in literature, and especially writers like Stephen Crane, Carl Sandburg, Jesse Stuart, and James A. Michener, it was meeting Maurice Dunbar on a cruise ship that turned my love of books into a second career. I'll never forget our meeting—it was on the S.S. Veendam of Holland America Line, a ship that still sails under another name and flag. We were dinnermates and a friendship was developed that first night that continues to flourish. In fact, I can say that it changed my life. I say this because I was about to retire from a long 25-year military career and was uncertain what I wanted to do with the rest of my life. I was burned out in medicine, at least the military version of it, as well as the private sector. I wanted to find something to do that I loved and at this point in my life it was hard to find anything of much interest.

I've had a lifelong interest in Stephen Crane, not just for the great books he wrote in his very short years (he was only 28 when he died in 1900), but because I once believed he could have been my grandfather. My father was born on the estate in Sussex, England where Crane spent his last three years. This was Brede Place, owned by Moreton Frewen (1850-1924), the Victorian adventurer who was Winston Churchill's uncle, and who was somewhat immortalized in James A. Michener's novel *Centennial.* However, I was to learn that I was not a descendant of Stephen Crane on my first visit to England during college in 1958, when I found that my father, born in 1894, was three years old when Crane first came to England in 1897. And while my search for identity ended then, my interest in Crane didn't wane; in fact, it increased to the point where I suppose I am now one of the leading authorities on Crane's life and works, as well as a major collector of his first and early editions.

It was Maurice Dunbar's book *Books and Collectors*, in its first and second editions, that is responsible for my now having a life as a book collector in which I never know boredom. From this book, I learned the essentials of book collecting, such as identifying first editions, and more importantly, to focus my collection on Crane and his times. It is often said that modern literature began on the pages of Crane's first novel *Maggie, a Girl of the Streets: A Story of New York.* Crane first wrote this book during the winter of 1892 and used money from his family to have it privately published. He wrote *Maggie* under the pseudonym of Johnston Smith. It was published in a dull yellow paper cover. Crane and his bohemian friends in New York City's Bowery of the 1890s thought the book would catch on and that the public would ask: "Who is Johnston Smith?" And Crane and his roommates planned that Crane would step out and announce that he and Johnston Smith were one and the same, resulting in fame and fortune. But it didn't happen that way—*Maggie,* Johnston Smith and Stephen Crane would never have become household words had it not been for Crane's second novel, the immortal *The Red Badge of Courage.* In fact, some biographers of Crane reported for generations that Crane and his cronies had burned all the copies of the baby-feces yellow paperback of *Maggie.*

And out of this comes one of the strangest true stories from the annals of book collecting in the last century. This is the case of the missing *Maggies,* as told by that stellar book collector, attorney, and scholar, David A. Randall, in his 1962 classic of bibliophilia, *Dukedom Large Enough* (Random House). Within a few months of meeting Maurice Dunbar, I traveled to his California home and on discussing Crane, he took me to meet Dr. Randall's son, Ron Randall, who has carried on the family tradition by running a top antiquarian bookstore in San Francisco.

It was the late David Randall who turned the book collectors and scholars on their noses by revealing that all the copies of Crane's yellow-papered *Maggies* were not burned. He reveals how a niece of Stephen Crane had at least a dozen of them stashed in a family attic in New Jersey and would conveniently put one at a rare book auction every few years. At first, the prices were sky high—a copy went for $3,100 in 1923 dollars, but on finding that there were others in a family cache, the price dropped to $75 a copy. Today, the price is over $10,000. Not bad for a poor quality, vanity-published book by a non-person that Crane named Johnston Smith.

Maggie prices are much higher than those for *The Red Badge of Courage,* Crane's true masterpiece. Without doubt, this novel of the American Civil War is one of the 10 great books of American literature. In fact, some authorities rank it among the greatest novels of all time. It made its first appearance in print in serialized form in the *Philadelphia Inquirer;* a chapter of the short novel was published each day.

While some have written that *The Red Badge* did not stir up much excitement when first published, there is clear, indisputable evidence that it most certainly did. On its publication day of October 5, 1895, it sold 4,500 copies at $1 each in its first few days, which may have been the entire first edition. It was published by D. Appleton and Company of New York, which almost immediately re-published Crane's earlier yellow paperback, *Maggie,* in a hardcover and under Crane's name. The publisher firmly denied that there had been an earlier edition of this story of a prostitute in New York's seamy Bowery. In a publisher's note on Page v of the first hardcover edition, Appleton's editors wrote:

> *As to this book which succeeds* The Red Badge of Courage, *it should be said that* Maggie *has never been published before, even in serial form. The story was put into type and copyrighted by Mr. Crane three years ago, but this real and strenuous tale of New York life is now given to the public for the first time.*

Both *Maggie* and *Red Badge* were printed in identical style in their first hardcover edition. The covers are in a yellow buckram with titles in the same red and black typeface and a red gilt figure at the top and bottom.   For the collector's interest, the first state of the first edition has no break in type on the word "congratulated" on the last line of Page 225, and the advertisements starting on Page 235 feature books by Gilbert Parker.

Crane collectors should also note that there is a great debate over whether the first state, first edition of *The Red Badge of Courage* had a dust jacket. No less an authority than the editors of the *First Edition Library* maintain it did not. And in their 1994 facsimile edition, it does not have a dust jacket. But a recent offering of a first edition, first printing of the book in a very reputable rare book dealer catalog, lists a copy "a little bumped, minor foxing to cover cloth and edges, otherwise fine in a dust jacket that is archivally backed with tissue, with some nicks and minor rubbing." And this catalog says more about the issue of dust jackets on first editions of *The Red Badge of Courage*:

> *The same printed dust jacket was used on subsequent printings of the original edition. While our information is anecdotal, and our conclusion may be hasty and thereby faulty, the jackets we have seen that are without*

doubt original to copies of the earliest printing have very long front flaps (like the present copy offered here) extending nearly to the inner front hinge. Later ones appear to be trimmed. Admittedly this observation is based on a small sample. Bibliographers have traditionally ignored dust jackets, reflecting the bias of earlier generations of collectors and booksellers against them. The monumental and authoritative Bibliography of American Literature *does not even mention **dust jackets, which like the books they wrap around, often have different printings, states and issues.** All in good time we suppose; a bibliographer once commented to us that every bibliography is a plea for information.* (Emphasis added.)

Also of interest is the price tag on this supposed first edition, first printing of *Red Badge*: $6,500.

But on second look with some study of authors of Crane's period and reputation, the $6,500 does not seem totally out-of-hand. For example, in the same catalog that lists the *Red Badge* is a first edition, first issue of Crane's fellow author and close friend, H. Rider Haggard's *King Solomon's Mines* (London: Cassell and Co., 1885) offered for $10,000; a first American edition of Jack London's *Adventure* (New York: Macmillan and Co., 1911) for $2,850; a Robert Louis Stevenson *Treasure Island* (London: Cassell and Co., 1883) first edition, first printing of 2,000 copies for $10,000; a first edition, first issue of Bram Stoker's *Dracula* (London: Archibald Constable, 1897) for $9,500; also a *Dracula* first American edition (New York: Doubleday & McClure, 1899) for $4,000; a Phineas Thayer (Ernest L.) first edition of *Casey at the Bat* (New York: Amsterdam Book Co., 1901) for $8,500; Lew Wallace's *Ben Hur: a Tale of the Christ* (New York: Harper & Bros., 1880) for $5,000 in dust jacket; a signed first edition of Oscar Wilde's *An Ideal Husband* (London: Leonard Smithers, 1899) for $4,500; Edgar Rice Burroughs' *Tarzan of the Apes* (Chicago: A.C. McClurg, 1914) for $50,000 in fine dust jacket; and a two-volume first English edition of Henry James' *Daisy Miller: An International Episode. Four Meetings* (London: Macmillan and Co., 1879) for $5,750.

When Stephen Crane first editions of any state come up for sale, I and the book's author can't help but recall one of our book-buying expeditions, where we found an entire 18-book collection of every Stephen Crane title and early edition (including a paperback *Maggie* by Johnston Smith in very good condition for this fragile book, and a first edition, first state of *Red Badge of Courage* in dust jacket for a price of just $12,500.

The *Maggie* copy went for $13,000 alone just five years later and the *Red Badge* copy is the one with the $6,500 price tag. And to make us even sicker that we didn't jointly buy this whole one-of-a-kind collection for $12,500, it also included copies of the extremely rare 1895 Copeland and Day vellum edition of Crane's little book of poetry, *Black Riders* (today's price: $1,500). We could probably have gotten the whole collection for $10,000, a virtual steal for a collection that was then broken up and sold in individual titles for at least four times the original asking price.

It is also a tragedy to see such a collection broken up—there can be no doubt that this collection would, in time, have been worth many times more. And more importantly, this collection of Crane's works was the largest and most complete in existence. Now it is gone—scattered to the four winds rather than being kept together for posterity. And the novels were all in their original dust jackets, too. This was truly the kind of nightmare that book collectors really dread witnessing. Our advice to fellow book lovers and collectors: Buy that collection you're looking at and can afford now—it may never come up for sale again as an intact collection.

An advantage of collecting Stephen Crane as well as other writers of his period and reputation is that there is a wide range of prices for his first and early editions, depending on the title. But wait a moment, you say, Crane died at 28 and didn't have other titles. In truth, Crane was one of the most prolific writers of all time. He wrote a dozen books, including seven novels (*Maggie, a Girl of the Streets; The Red Badge of Courage; George's Mother; The Monster; Active Service;* and *The O'Ruddy,* in which Crane wrote 27 chapters and Robert Barr wrote the concluding seven chapters). His large number of short stories and essays were to be published only in part in six book-length collections (*The Little Regiment, The Open Boat, The Whilomville Stories, Great Battles of the World,* and

Last Words, published posthumously). And finally, he also had two books of important milestone poetry published, *Black Riders* and *War is Kind*. What a prodigious literary output for a man who died at 28!

My collection includes all of Crane's first editions except *Last Words*, four of them personally inscribed by Crane, including one to none other than Winston Churchill, who was less than three years younger than Crane.

Perhaps I should explain that Crane spent his last three years of life in literary exile, say some, or in a literary Valhalla, say others. He made his home in a 13th century Norman manor house in Sussex called Brede Place, which he leased from his fellow late Victorian adventurer, Moreton Frewen, who was later to be called Mortal Ruin for his disastrous series of financial schemes, none of which ever made him more than debts. Frewen had met Crane during Frewen's so-called American period, when he made more than 100 trips to America between 1876 and 1919 meeting important people and literary figures such as Crane. During his three final years in England and Ireland, Crane hob-nobbed with the top level of society as well as the literary lions of his time, including H.G. Wells, Henry James, Rider Haggard, Ford Madox Ford, Harold Frederic and Joseph Conrad. All lived in close proximity to Brede Place and Crane and his common-law wife, Cora, gave memorable parties for these great writers.

These English years and their hundreds of literary and historical associations helped me to expand my collection of Crane to include other writers of Crane's period, including such giants as the Lincoln biographer, folk singer, Pulitzer poet and historian Carl Sandburg, who met Crane briefly in Puerto Rico during the Spanish American War and modeled his writing on the quixotic and tragic Crane. And from Sandburg came my interest in other writers such as Jesse Stuart, author of the great group of poems entitled *Man with a Bull Tongue Plow* and 38 other books in a literary career that spanned half a century and touched thousands of students' lives, and finally into the present, the world's greatest storyteller, James A. Michener. It was my privilege to know these three great writers personally, and to also become a collector of their books along with those of Stephen Crane, the literary father of them all.

Then I started finding all kinds of Crane connections to others he met—which continues to expand my collection. First, I began to collect books and memorabilia of those who knew Crane, such as Lt. Gen. Nelson Appleton Miles, the Medal of Honor Civil War veteran who became a two-star boy general at the age of 24 (along with George Armstrong Custer and other so-called boy wonders of the U.S. Civil War). Miles got to know Crane during the Spanish American War, especially during the invasion of Puerto Rico (which Gen. Miles made certain would not be a near disaster as the Cuban campaign became). I even have a book that Crane autographed to Miles, who was to become the last soldier to hold the title that Winfield Scott, Ulysses S. Grant, William T. Sherman and Phillip Sheridan held: Commanding General of the U.S. Army. The U.S. went to a staff system in which the Army chief was titled Chief of Staff, after Gen. Miles was forced to retire by Teddy Roosevelt, who had deeply resented Miles since San Juan Hill and the Roughriders. (Teddy didn't get along with Crane either, both for his truthful war dispatches from Cuba and for his earlier work in New York. T.R. was police commissioner during Crane's research of the poverty and ills of urban life from the Bowery—*Maggie* and a group of powerful short stories being the fruition of this period in Crane's career.)

Many a long night I sat up with Jesse Stuart, both a major American writer and educator, in his rustic West Hollow, Ky. mansion, listening to the mountain poet tell of how he was inspired by the word colorings of emotions and free verse poetry of Stephen Crane. Though Crane was more than a generation before Stuart, the Crane connection was made through Carl Sandburg, who had personally met Crane in Puerto Rico and had an inscribed copy of *George's Mother* with him until he died. That volume is now in my Crane collection. And James Michener has told me hours of accounts of his debt to writers such as Crane and Sandburg.

My collections of Crane, Sandburg, Stuart and Michener continue to grow. I now have 186 separate editions and printings of *The Red Badge of Courage,* including 29 in foreign languages. I also have a number of prize Crane letters, along with many from Carl Sandburg, Jesse Stuart and James Michener. And the joy is that this is an endless pursuit—I'll never find all the editions, the various reprints, the inscribed book, the clipped magazine article, or the dispatch or anecdote. It is a life of books and with them, I have learned that I shall never know boredom.

And who knows, I may yet find that copy of Crane's *Last Words* that's been eluding me for so many years of searching. And it might be right there in that corner of the quaint little bookstore in Ireland, in a Sussex or Kent village near where Crane lived at Brede Place, or even at a hometown flea market. That's the joy of book collecting, one of the greatest and most satisfying activities known to Man since he came out of the trees and caves.

BOOK COLLECTING ON THE WEB

BY DENNIS M. TAUGHER

WILL COMPUTERS REPLACE books? The media and Internet hype-meisters would like you to believe so. The Internet is being touted to cure all ills, including warts. We will soon be reading Tolstoy, de Tocqueville, Danielle Steel and Harold Robbins using our computers. Do you really believe this? If you do, I have a bridge I'd like to sell you.

Books as we know them are here to stay. And let me predict, books will not be replaced by any digital medium in our lifetimes. Holding a book and reading text on a computer screen are two different experiences. Both have value, but how would you like to curl up by a fireplace with a cup of tea...and a good book on your computer screen? Screens are small and not easy on the eyes for extended periods of time. A book is small and portable. Books can provide an immense amount of pleasure when you just hold or look at them. They not only transmit ideas, but can be objects of beauty, especially with fine binding or a terrific dust jacket. You can't say the same about your computer screen.

So although the computer won't replace the book, the computer can play a valuable role in the life of the book collector. Without a computer, your book collecting expeditions are limited by geography and time. But with a computer, you can access book dealers and fellow collectors around the world—without leaving your home.

In the next page or so, I'll discuss how computer users can use the Internet to help them in their book collecting efforts. If you're an experienced Internet user, you'll probably want to skip ahead to the section titled "Internet Resources for Book Collectors."

GETTING STARTED ON THE INTERNET

To get telephone service, you must have a telephone, a line connecting you to the network, and a hookup through your local carrier. The Internet works the same way. You need the proper equipment—in this case, a computer instead of a telephone. You also need a line. You can get a direct hookup to the Internet by installing an ISDN line. However, the average home user relies on a modem, which allows your computer to use your home's telephone wiring. (Get the fastest one you can afford, such as a 28,800 or 36,600 baud—the time you'll save will more than justify the extra cost over a cheaper, slower modem.) Finally, just as you have to select AT&T, Sprint, MCI or whatever to provide your service, you need to select an Internet service provider.

The easiest way for neophytes to access the Net is through one of the online services, such as America Online, CompuServe or Prodigy. These services offer on-line chat rooms and loads of exclusive information (movie reviews, investment information), as well as access to the Net. I suggest starting with one of these.

AT&T and some of the "Baby Bells" also offer Internet access. The cost is minimal, usually less than $20 per month for a limited number of hours, with additional hours at a reduced rate. If you're not ready to make such an investment at this time, check with family members or friends or neighbors who have Internet access and ask them to take you on a tour of the Net. Many local libraries also offer Internet access. If your library provides this service, it's a great way to explore the Internet before making a sizable investment in equipment. However, I've found it's worth getting access to the Internet just to send e-mail. It's fast and cheap and everybody's doing it. My entire family (including my 83-year-old mother) all use e-mail.

SEARCHING THE INTERNET

Now that you have access to the Internet, what next? Special software programs, called "browsers," make it easier to navigate the Internet — you simply have to click on icons (graphic images) or type in the Internet "addresses" to find the site you want. Many newer computers come loaded with browser software, and if you sign up with an online service, it will provide you with a browser program. (Netscape and Microsoft Explorer are two of the most popular.) The best place to start your book-collecting research is the World Wide Web (known as the Web), which is a special portion of the Internet devoted to commercial transactions. Unlike the rest of the Internet, which relies on text-based user interfaces, the Web allows you to view graphics and animation as well as text. You can even hear audio clips.

Millions of businesses have taken advantage of the capabilities of the World Wide Web to set up Web sites, which are a sort of electronic storefront. The Web is a veritable gold mine for book collectors, with a wealth of sites from antiquarian, used and specialty book dealers.

Every Web site has a "universal resource locator," or URL, which serves as its address on the Web. By typing in this string of alphanumeric characters (which usually starts with "http://www") in the appropriate window on your browser, your browser will locate the site and download the information it contains in a readable format on your computer screen. But if you don't know a Web site's URL, how can you find it? While it's not as easy as looking in your local yellow pages under "books," special tools called "search engines" can help you find the Web sites that interest you.

Some of the most popular search engines are:

- Alta Vista: http://altavista.digital.com/. One of the most powerful and comprehensive search engines available; great for business uses.

- Yahoo!: http://www.yahoo.com/. This pioneering search engine allows keyword searches, as well as searches in one of several general topic areas. More consumer-oriented than other sites; lots of ads and special features.

- Lycos: http://www.lycos.com/. Offers custom search capabilities, reviews of Web sites, etc. An interesting feature offered by this site is that it allows you to search the Web by picture or sounds rather than text only.

- InfoSeek: http://www.infoseek.com/. Offers searches by "specific question, phrase or name," as well as allowing you to browse several topic-specific directories.

- WebCrawler: http://www.webcrawler.com/. Search engine allows you to get list of relevant site titles or summaries. One very interesting feature WebCrawler offers is called "searching the Web backwards," which allows you to find the sites linked to a specific site. Find out what sites have links to your favorite book dealer—who knows what you'll find?

- Excite!: http://www.excite.com/. Offers advanced search capabilities, Web site reviews, "sightseeing tours," and more.

- Magellan: http://www.mckinley.com/. Offers two search options: a search of sites that have been rated and reviewed only, or a search of the entire Magellan database.

- Savvy Search: http://savvy.cs.colostate.edu:2000/ (Note there is no www in the address.) Allows you to query nearly 30 (at last count) search engines simultaneously, with one entry.

- All4One Search Machine: http://all4one/ (Note there is no www in the address.) Allows you to query four search engines simultaneously.

- Search.Com: http://www.search.com. Like the preceding two sites, allows you to query more than one search engine simultaneously. Also offers an "internal search tool," which can help you find the right tool to find the exact information you want.

Let's try a search and see what we get. I experimented with each of the search engines listed above. One of the problems with the search engines is there is no standard format of categorizing information, like the Dewey decimal system. You have to work with a search engine for a while to get a feel for how it works. I first tried "books collectible." Taugher Books, my website, came up on Lycos and Yahoo. I then typed in "Taugher Books" and found it listed on Web Crawler and Magellan. One of the most interesting I used was Savvy Search. You can search four search engines at once with one entry.

A word of advice: do your searches during off-peak hours on the Internet. Otherwise the download time will be slow or connections will be refused.

It's difficult to say which one of these search engines is best. I suggest you try them all. Then choose one or two that give you the best results. My hope is that somebody will standardize the search categories and make our lives a bit easier.

BUYING AND SELLING BOOKS ON THE NET

Now you're on the Internet and getting familiar with its vast resources for book collectors. Here's the main question—what's it like to buy and sell books over the Net?

There are currently two "marketplaces" where you can post general messages and messages on books wanted and for sale. The first one is reached through a newsgroup called Usenet. Go to the address: rec.arts.books.marketplace. There may be as many as 500+ messages. You can post a message that every other user has access to, if they choose to read it. To get your message read by the appropriate audience, make sure to give it a descriptive title. For example, if you have a first edition of Steinbeck's *Grapes of Wrath* you want to sell, the title, "Book for sale" is unlikely to attract Steinbeck collectors. But the title "Steinbeck first edition for sale" would attract the attention of any Steinbeck collector who happened to be perusing the Usenet.

The other "marketplace" is a ListServe called Bibliophile. It's similar to an automatic subscription service. You sign up (biblio@smartlink.net), using the instructions. The ListServe will respond saying you are now a subscriber. Thereafter, you will receive every message posted. Beware! It's possible to get several hundred messages in a few days. It's a good idea to unsubscribe before going on vacation or out of town. Bibliophile is mainly a place to buy and sell books, but there are often lively discussions. Any one can post a question and someone will usually respond.

My experience of selling on the Net has been very positive. My home page (http://www.batnet.com/taugher/) has a series of links. For example, you can download the index of my inventory or go to the top or bottom of any particular page. I also have pages for my business policies and a form to send me e-mail. There are also links to other dealers.

People have been able to find my home page, browse it and send me e-mail or call. I respond if I have the book and send an e-mail copy of my business policies. Since I offer credit card payment, people feel comfortable buying from me. They are protected from fraud.

Selling books to collectors in other countries used to be a challenge. Phone calls are expensive and time differences difficult to work around. But the Internet has changed all that. People can send inquiries and conduct the entire transaction by e-mail. If they pay by credit card they not only get their books faster, but get the best exchange rate.

Here are the experiences of several other sellers and buyers:

Ed Smith of Ed Smith Books, Oak View, Calif. "I love the Net and do quite well on it. We have a catalog on the ABAA's page. We also post on Biblio and rec.arts.books.marketplace. We are now setting up our own home page. What I love most about it is the SPEED of the thing. When the fax came out, we thought it was THE tool. Now, we have the ultimate machine. It reaches out there to everyone who has access to a computer."

Barbara Levy. "What I like best is there are so many dealers out there that I would not know of if I didn't have access to the Internet. You don't have to worry about business hours, because you can just e-mail to reserve books and get info. . . When I asked for a detailed description of a book, I got one, right down to the minutest smudge."

Gerard Gromley, Manchester-by-the-Sea, Mass. "I love everything about selling books on the Internet—the immediacy of communication, the dialogue with collectors and dealers, the worldwide scope of the Net. We and our UK friends are very fortunate that so many people the world over are fluent in English. I am often surprised to find that a customer, with whom I have been exchanging e-mail for days, lives in another country."

INTERNET RESOURCES FOR BOOK COLLECTORS

While no means complete, comprehensive or even representative of the huge number of Internet sites waiting to be explored, here's a list of a few that might be of interest to book collectors. (This list was current at time of press; however, things change rapidly on the Internet. If you can't find a Web site under the URL listed, you can try one of the search engines.)

ABAA Booknet. URL = http://www.rmharris.com/pub/abaa-booknet

This is the Antiquarian Booksellers' Association of America (ABAA) site, which has nearly 200 booksellers online. Visitors can find dealers by specialty or location and search through their catalogs. Other features include a schedule of book fairs and regional shows and "Book Security," which allows collectors and dealers to report stolen books and forgeries by filing a loss report, which will be forwarded to ABAA dealers.

Antiquarian Book Shops and Associations. URL = http://www.connectotel.com/books/wwwbs.htm.

Contains an alphabetical list of antiquarian book shops and associations. Worldwide in scope.

Amazon Bookstore. URL = http://www.amazon.com.

This is the site of Seattle-based Amazon Books, "the world's largest bookstore," which boasts one million titles. The Web site is as comprehensive as its catalog of offerings, including the following features:

· catalog, searchable by author, title, subject or keyword

· "shelf browser," which lets you look at editors' favorite titles and customers' reviews

· "eyes" personal notification service, an automated searcher which will send you e-mail when the books you want are published (you can specify author or topic)

· "register with editors," a service that allows you to have one or more of 40 editors who specialize in certain topics notify you when books you want are published

· publishers pages.

Bibliophile Homepage. URL = http://www.auldbooks.com/biblio/index.html

Includes:

· events calendar—international listing of book fairs and shows

· Biblio Book School (articles on various aspects of selling and collecting books)

· search capabilities—allows visitors to search participating dealers by specialty, location, name, or proprietor(s)

· bibliography, including online resources and other good stuff

· mailing list "maintained for the benefit of sellers and/or collectors of rare, out-of-print, [and] scarce books in all subject areas." Subscribe by sending an e-mail message to "biblio-request@smartlink.net." The body of your message should read "subscribe" (without quotes).

Bookport. URL = http://www.bookport.com/b_welcomehome.html

Includes:

· Publishers index: publishers on the World Wide Web, publishers offering WWW ordering of bound books, publishers offering online editions. Search by name or keyword.

· Booksellers directory—directory of booksellers on Web

· Bookfairs and festivals—calendar listing, plus mailing list so you can receive listings of fairs

· Recent discoveries of editors—books and other items of interest to bibliophiles.

Internet Book Information Center. URL = http://sunsite.unc.edu/ibic/IBIC-homepage.html

Includes:

· Reviews and news about books (primarily new books)

· IBIC Guide to Book-Related Resources on the Internet

· List of USENET book-related discussion groups—from the otherworldly (Asimov) to the ridiculous (Limbaugh)

The Great Northwest Bookstore. URL = http://www.teleport.com/~gnwdt/list.html

A used book store with 150,000 titles, the site includes a catalog and glossary of 20 book collecting terms and related links.

Association des Bibliophiles Universels. URL = http://web.cnom.fr/ABU/

Text is primarily in French, with main portions translated into English. Visitors can locate online versions of rare books from various archives around the world, some with illustrations.

Kennys Bookshop and Art Galleries. URL = http://www.iol.ie/resource/Kennys/welcome.html

Site maintained by Kennys Bookshop of Galway, Ireland, specialists in new and antiquarian books of Irish interest. Includes online catalog, billed as "the most comprehensive catalog of Irish books in the world."

Mail order bookstores (list). URL = ftp://rtfm.mit.edu/pub/usenet/news.answers/books/stores/ship-by-mail. Or send e-mail to mail-server@rtfm.mit.edu. In body of message type "send usenet/news.answers/books/stores/ship-by-mail" (without quotes).

A useful list of "physical" bookstores that do mail order through the World Wide Web. List arranged by topic.

Moe's Books. URL = http://moesbooks.com/moe.htm

Berkeley, Calif.-based seller of used and antiquarian books.

Virtual Book Shop. URL = http://www.virtual.bookshop.com/

"Specializing in rare, first edition, antiquarian, collectible and fine books provided by many of the world's finest booksellers."

Includes online catalog, searchable by author, title, subject or description.

Asian Rare Books. URL = http://www.columbia.edu/cu/ccs/cuwl/clients/arb/

Catalogs and ordering via e-mail.

Ventura Pacific. URL = http://www.fishnet.net/~sandcat/photo.htm

Specializing in photographic books, including used and first editions. Offers e-mail ordering with Visa or MasterCard.

Sandcat. URL = http://www.fishnet.net/~sandcat/

This site bills itself as "a virtual treasure hunt for collectors." Includes a listing of rare and first edition books by category, including art, Western, rock music, photography, sports, science fiction, children's collectible, cookbooks and wine guides, vintage paperbacks. Also offers a "bookfinders service"; access it by sending an e-mail message to "sandcat@fishnet.com."

There is a treasure trove of books waiting to be found on the Internet. Today's Internet is like a Wild West town: very few rules or laws. Things get done by individual effort. So, fire up your modem and grab the next wave. Happy Surfing!

Taugher Books specializes in modern first editions, detective fiction, books on book collecting and black literature. We regularly issue catalogs and are open by appointment. Check out our inventory on the World Wide Web at: http://www.batnet.com/taugher/

SIZE OF BOOKS OR FORMAT

To go beyond the bounds of moderation is to outrage humanity.

—Blaise Pascal

A FOLIO (Latin, "leaf") is a full-sized sheet of printer's paper (or vellum or any other writing material). In a folio-size book, each has been folded once. In a quatro-size, each sheet has been folded twice, and in octavo, three times. The sizes then are respectively one-half, one quarter, and one eighth of the size of the original sheet. This would all be very simple and standardized except for the fact that the sizes of the original sheets vary greatly. Theoretically, the folio sheet could be of any size imaginable. There is a book called the *Super Book* published in Denver, Colorado in 1976 that measures 9 feet by 10 feet 2-1/8 inches, and which, with 300 pages, weighs 557 lbs. The following describes the world's smallest book:

> *The smallest bound book with cursive material print-ed in moveable metal type (as opposed to any micro-pho-tographic process) is one of 3.5 mm by 3.5 mm (0.14 by 0.14 inches) printed for the Gutenburg Museum, Mainz, West Germany. It contains the Lord's Prayer in 7 languages.*[42]

---

[42]Norris Mc Whirter, ed., *Guinness Book of World Records* (New York: Sterling Publ. Co., Inc., 1979). p. 209.

However, the standard products of the publishers provide variety enough without resorting to freaks, as the following chart will show.

SIZES OF FOLIOS		
Abbreviations	*Name of Folios*	*Measurement (inches)*
Atl.	Atlas	34 x 26
El.	Elephant	28 x 23
Imp.	Imperial	30 x 22
Sup. Roy.	Super Royal	27 1/2 x 20 1/2
Roy.	Royal	25 x 20
Med.	Medium	23 x 18
—	Demy	22 1/2 x 17 1/2
Cr.	Crown	20 x 15
—	Post	19 1/4 x 15 1/2
F'cap.	Foolscap	17 x 13 1/2

The format (size) of a book, determined from the size of the folio (original sheet) and the number of times the sheet has been folded, has nothing to do with the thickness of the book, i.e., the number of pages. So we may have a "tk 4°" (thick quarto) or a "thin 8°" (thin octavo) or any combination.

The following indicates the abbreviations employed by printers for formats:

Fo., fol., 2°	Folio
Qto., 4to, 4°	Quarto
Oct., 8vo, 8°	Octavo
12mo, 12°	Duodecimo
16mo, 16°	Sextodecimo
24mo, 24°	Vicesimo-quarto

And so on, practically *ad infinitum*. Books smaller in format than 12mo are usual and in recent printings, rare. Bookmen say "quarto" and "octavo" but past that, they say "twelve-mo" and "sixteen-mo", and so on.

So the format (quarto, octavo, etc.) factor is only the roughest kind of indication of the actual dimensions of a book. As you can see from the charts, a foolscap folio would not differ greatly from an atlas quarto.

Other factors being equal, such as quality of paper, the larger the book, the more expensive to manufacture. However, in the used book market, size has almost nothing to do with value. So don't be impressed by the sheer size of a volume. As a matter of fact, huge books are a pain in the ischial tuberosities. You can't handle them on the john, in the car, on a plane or a bus, and you can't read them in bed. They are a nuisance to store. Their dust jackets (if any) are difficult to maintain and awkward to cover with clear plastic covers. Lying on a beautiful coffee table, they may impress the guests, but they are not very useful.

In appearance, a folio is a large upright book, taller perhaps by a half than its width. An octavo is a small upright book, and a quarto is somewhere in between. Some books are square in shape. This aberration is most commonly seen in quarto books. Fortunately, there aren't very many books produced in the square configuration as it is a most awkward volume to handle and store. Odd size and over-sized books are a gripe and nuisance when trying to arrange a collection chronologically or by genre. Because of its convenient shape and size, there are probably more octavo format books in existence than all other combined. The size of the book in hand is an average octavo.

THE COLLECTOR IN CONCLUSION

BOREDOM—HAVING NOTHING to do—is among the most insidious of human discomforts and causes of unhappiness. It may be a major factor in crime and delinquency, especially among the youth. Boredom may well contribute to much alcohol and drug abuse. With the burgeoning development of automation and the consequent increase in leisure time, the boredom factor is not apt to diminish. What are we going to do with all that leisure time? The summer vacation of the schools is a vestige of the time when children were needed to help harvest the crops. But now when one man in a diesel-powered air-conditioned CB-radio equipped combine can do the work of a whole rural village of former times, what is there for the youth to do?

It took mankind thousands of years of toil and ingenuity to achieve the 40-hour week (less than 40 hours for many already) and now, for the most part, he doesn't know what to do with the time remaining after the work week is fulfilled. The issue of leisure is a formidable one with vast ramifications. With machines to do the menial and the repetitive, people are freed from such time-consuming labor. Free to do what?

Challenging, intellectually stimulating hobbies such as book collecting might prove to be instrumental in resolving the problem of leisure. There is nothing exclusive about book collecting. There is no reason why one engaged in that hobby could not also be involved in philately, numismatics, painting, weaving, photography, wood working, horticulture, or any of the vast number of activities. Book collecting can be a primary hobby, or it can be an ancillary or "service" hobby. For example, the gardener could collect a working library of books about botany, herbicides and pesticides, decorative horticulture, historical works, etc.

In any case, it seems a safe conjecture that the hobbyist of whatever preference may be markedly better equipped to handle his ever-increasing leisure time. Retired persons confront this problem from the day they receive the gold watch. Those who have cultivated absorbing interests over the years delight in their retirement. In fact, finding something to do is usually the least of their problems. I am reminded of an ironworker in his middle fifties who has a number of organized interests—stamp collecting, painting, reading, and gourmet cooking. A man who quit school in the ninth grade, he has never allowed the lack of diplomas to limit either his learning or his interests. His retirement will never be boring to him. However, those whose time has been consumed by work, more work, and television often have much heavy time on their hands when they punch the clock for the last time.

Go to a coin collector's show-and-sale or just read *Stamps*, the weekly magazine of philately. Attend an antiques show. Observe the people with their beautiful booths of Depression glass, brass artifacts, porcelain, toby jugs, jewelry, china, furniture, etc. Most such antiques-and-collectibles fairs feature books, too. Meet the people participating in the show. You will never find more interesting and interested men and women. They have something to do and they love doing it. If they have a gripe at all, it is invariably that there is not enough time in a day. Most of them belong to various organizations appropriate to their specialties. One example is the Questors Club, devoted to learning and teaching about antiques of all sorts. This and other good organizations conduct meetings, some have annual conventions, publish special, journals, do research, and interact with collectors and dealers.

Purposeful living characterizes the active hobbist, the serious amateur,[43] as opposed to aimless. You will rarely find him wandering the streets, hustling the bars, or cluttering up the courts and jails. He is too busy searching, corresponding, calling, and studying to be wasting his time in dissipation. He is too busy to feel sorry for himself. He is busy making a living, obeying the laws, paying his bills and his taxes—and being responsible. He is the cadre of civilization and the crosstie of the rails of history.

One of the most productive, creative, wide and useful lives ever spent on earth was that of Benjamin Franklin. Scientist, inventor, innovator, revolutionary, diplomat, writer, and sage, he always identified himself as a printer. Always the craftsman, the professional printer, he was an *amateur* in at least a dozen disciplines, many of them demanding the highest order of ability. Although written when he was only 22, his famous epitaph was just as valid 62 years later at the time of his death. Perhaps it is a fitting thought for living amateurs.

The body

of

BENJAMIN FRANKLIN

printer

(Like the cover of an old book,

its contents torn out,

And stripped of its lettering and gliding)

Lies here, food for worms.

Yet the work itself will not be lost

For it will, as he believed, appear once more

In a new

And more beautiful edition,

Corrected and amended

by

THE AUTHOR

---

[43]One who engages in any recognized discipline as a pastime rather than as a profession. A French word derived from Latin *amator*, a lover. Thus one who does something as a devotion, a love. Not to be interpreted, in this book at least, as unskillful or superficial. If I wanted to know something about Dickens, for example, I would not call a professional teacher of literature. I would call a certain chemist who is a Dickens amateur.

GLOSSARY

The finest words in the world are only vain sounds if you cannot comprehend them

—Anatole France

A "GLOSS" IS an interlineary or marginal explanation deriving from Latin *glossa*, from the Greek word for "tongue" (language). A glossary is a collection of glosses. The book world—publishers, printers, dealers, collectors, and librarians—has accumulated a specialized vocabulary much as other trades, crafts, and professions have done. To understand the vocabulary of a specialized discipline is to make significant progress in mastering that discipline.

ana	A morpheme (suffix) denoting that the material in question is about a particular subject—Californiana, Sherlockiana, boxiana, Victoriana, Scaligeriana.
Antiquarian books	An antiquary was the official custodian or recorder of antiquities (a title bestowed by Henry VIII on John Leland). An antiquarian is therefore one who is a student and/or collector of the desirable and old. Generally, books that are old (over 150 years) and collectable.

Association copy	A book that has been associated with or has some special relationship to a well-known person. William Dean Howell's personal copy of Lowell's *Among my Books* would be a Howell's association copy. Association copies must have some means of positive identification—bookplates, signatures, name stamps, letters, etc. Association copies can be valuable even in cases where the book has little intrinsic value.
Biblioklept	A book thief. One of the worst forms of subhuman depravity. A facetious term.
Bibliomanic	A victim of the obsessive-compulsive neurosis characterized by a congested library and an atrophied bank account. A condition promoted by booksellers and cronies and deplored by spouses. A term made famous by Eugene Field in his *The Love Affairs of a Bibliomaniac*, published in 1896. An abandoned fanatic.
Bibliophile	A book lover, usually a collector, a victim of a markedly less acute and debilitating condition than that of the bibliomaniac.
Bibliophobe	Someone married to a bibliophile. Bibliophobia does not seem to be infectious in etiology but appears to be precipitated by living with a bibliophile, or worse yet, a bibliomaniac. A severe reversal reaction, often self-preservative in nature.
Blind-stamped	Physical impressions or indentations on the binding of a book, countersunk and not inked or gilded. BOMC book are usually blind-stamped on the lower right hand corner of the back board.
Boards	The rigid covering of a book. Boards may be covered with a variety of materials—leather, cloth, vellum, etc. When paper only covers the boards, a book is said to be "in boards."
Bookplate	Any label or printed device carrying the identification of the owner and (usually) affixed to the

front pastedown. Plates vary from custom tooled leather or metal foil to cheap mass-produced paper printings. Some plates are custom designed by famous artists. There is a flourishing bookplate-collecting hobby and whole books on the subject.

Breaking copy A book that is taken apart to obtain illustrations or plates which may be sold individually and possibly framed. Usually a breaking copy is in sad shape and hardly collectable except for the plates.

Broadside An unfolded sheet with printing on one side only. Handbills and theater playbills are broadsides.

Browning Discoloration of the paper of a book. Characteristic of cheaply manufactured books. The Triangle Books and Blue Ribbon Books are typical examples. Severely browned paper is extremely brittle and will break or chip easily. Avoid badly browned books. Browning indicates more than just aging; it is chemical decomposition of the paper.

Calf A beautiful and durable leather made from calf-skin which will accept any color of dye. Tree calf has a design of the grain that is supposed to look like a tree but more closely resembles wood grain.

Called for "Bearing the intrusive dot between the 8's of p. 88 (in the 1st issue of *Of Mice and Men*) as called for in Goldstone & Payne." A term indicating that special information is necessary for the authentication of the status of a book and is available in an authoritative work.

Cancel Any part of a book used as a substitute for an original part of the book.

Cancelland(um) The original sheet or leaf is called the cancelland or cancellandum. That which is printed to replace it is called the cancel or cancellands.

Cap	The rounded tops and bottoms of the spines of books bound in leather. The top is the headcap; the bottom is the tailcap.
Cased	As contrasted to *bound*. In cased books, the covered boards are made up separately in numbers estimated to equal the number of books in the printing. The stitched quires are held together by the mull (a canvas strip) which is glued on the backs of the quires. Then these are inserted in to the case by machinery.
	Casing bears the same relationship to binding as ready-to-wear clothing bears to custom tailoring. Almost all of the books you are apt to see in new or used book stores will be cased.
Chapbooks	Single sheets like broadsides could be folded to make small booklets. From the 17th through the 19th centuries, such little booklets were sold on the streets by chapmen, i.e., sellers.
Chipped	Usually refers to spines or dust jackets. A book or d.j. is chipped if pieces of the material are broken off and missing. Browned d.j.'s are especially susceptible to chipping.
Colophon	Originally the colophon (Greek: "summit or finishing touch") was a statement placed at the back of the book indicating details of author, printer place and date of printing, etc. Early books had no title pages (q.v.) and colophons served to convey the information now found on title and copyright pages. Printers often put their trademarks with the colophon and when the trademarks came to be placed on the title pages, they were called colophons. The colophon of the Viking Press is a Viking ship. That of Knopf is the borzoi hounds.
Copyright page	The verso of the title page which conveys information consisting of the name of the copyright holder, the publisher, date of publication, date and number of printings. It is the copyright page that is most helpful in determining the edi-

tion of a book. Many publishers simply state "First Printing" or "First Edition." Information on the printer and binder is sometimes given at the bottom of the copyright page.

Cut
Edges of a book that are smooth and uniform, as opposed to "uncut" books that have an irregular rough appearance of the edges. See "uncut" and "unopened."

Deckled edge
Also called "feather edge." The rough edge of paper formed in a frame or deckle. In modern books, the deckled edge is usually confined to limited editions (see entry) and fine press books.

Dedication copy
A book presented by the author to the person to whom the book has been dedicated. *Travels with Charley* is dedicated to Harold Guinzburg, so his is the dedication copy.

Defective copy
A book from which something significant is lacking. A page or a plate is missing, for example.

Device
The trademark of the printer or publisher. Typical of modern devices would be the borzoi (Russians wolfhounds of Alfred A. Knopf, Inc.)

Doctored copy
A book that has been altered presumably to make it more desirable or valuable. Always used in a pejorative sense, the term indicates changes beyond mere cleaning, repairing, or restoring. There is more than a nuance of fraudulent practice in "doctoring" a book.

Dust jacket
The paper protective wrapper of a book. See the several pages in the text on this subject.

Edition princeps
Latin: "First Edition." A term reserved for the first book form of a work that had been in circulation in manuscript before the invention of moveable type printing.

Edition, first
Please refer to the special chapter on first editions, impressions, states, and printings.

End papers

These are the leaves at the front and back of the book which are not part of the prefatory material or the text. Paste-down end papers are secured to the boards. Free end papers are simply blank leaves. End papers may be decorated or a different color than the text. The first edition of *The Grapes of Wrath* has decorated end papers with the "Battle Hymn of the Republic" motif.

Extra-illustrated

A unique copy usually of a particularly desirable book which some booklover has laboriously tipped in or had re-bound into the book illustrations in addition to those originally published with the book. An example is the William Glyde Wilkins *Pickwick Papers* now in Dickens House in Palo Alto, Calif.

Facsimile

A legitimate copy, usually of a very rare or expensive book, made to appear as much like the original as practical. The Norton facsimile of the Shakespeare Folio is one example. A facsimile is not a fake, fraud, or forgery.

Fake

The result of the attempt of a forger to produce a book that will pass as a rare and expensive book. Thomas J. Wise (d. 1937) was the most successful of forgers. Ironically, some of his forgeries fetch higher prices than the originals that he forged.

Fore-edge paintings

Watercolor paintings applied to the fanned-out fore edge of a book. The fore or front edge is opposite the spine. In the normal position of a book, the paintings are invisible. They can only be seen when the edges are fanned out to present the broadest surface. Double fore-edge paintings are those that are made on opposite edges of the pages, i.e., there is one picture when fanned out in one direction, and another picture when spread out in the opposite direction.

The world's richest and most varied assemblage of fore-edge paintings (book) is in the Doheny

	Collection at St. John's Seminary, Camarillo, Calif. There are 614 fore edge books in the collection including about fifty double fore-edge paintings.[44]
Foxing	Reddish or rusty freckles on paper probably caused by uneven distribution of chemicals, particularly bleach, in the manufacture of the paper. "Some foxing," a note often seen in catalogs, seldom indicates a really inferior copy. The word may derive from the color of the red fox.
Frontispiece	An illustration, usually a portrait, facing the title page.
Galley proofs	A galley is the printer's type tray. Galley proofs are early type proofs and come in long strips. Highly prized by collectors, they constitute a part of the complete canon of a book. The Dept. of Special Collections at Stanford has the complete canon, including galley proofs, of *Cannery Row*.
Grangerized copy	In 1769 James Granger published a *Biographical History of England* with blank leaves for the reception of engraved portraits or other pictorial illustrations of the text. The filling up of a "Granger" became a favorite hobby and afterwards other books were treated in the same manner.
	Quoted from the *New York Tribune* of January 13, 1889: "The portraits of actors will be paged separately with blank backs, for the benefit of the Grangerizers."
Half-binding	Usually half leather. Such books ordinarily have the spine and a part of the boards covered with leather and some have the corners also covered.
Half title	A leaf in front of the book carrying only the title.

---

[44]For further information, see Carl J. Weber's *A Thousand and One Fore-Edge Paintings* (Waterville, Me., 1949).

Hinge	The area where the spine joins the board, functioning in a manner similar to the hinge on a casket, trunk, or on a door. Because of the hinge's being the site of the only motion or action involved in a book, this is where damage occurs first and most frequently. "Hinge starting" or "Hinge cracked" are common notes in catalogs.
Holograph	Greek: *holo*, "whole" and *graph*, "writing." A document written entirely in the handwriting of the author whose signature it usually bears. It is, of course, possible to have a "holograph letter" or note unsigned.
Incunabula	The Latin phrase *ab incunabulis* is literally "from the cradle." Concerning books published from the invention of printing, c. 1455 through the year 1500, i.e., the "cradle" of printing.
	The Morgan Library in New York and the Huntington Library in San Marino, Calif. both have magnificent collections of incunabula.
Juveniles	Books intended for young readers roughly from age 12 to young adulthood. Children's books are designed for the youngest readers, which books merge into the juveniles. There are no clear-cut boundaries as to where one leaves off and the other begins.
	("Adult," as applied to books recently, is a dishonest euphemism for pornographic books appealing to prurient interests.)
	Typical of the older juveniles are the Bobbsey Twins books, Tom Swift, and the Horatio Alger books.
Juvenilia	A writer's youthful works. "Thanatopsis" is part of the juvenilia of William Cullen Bryant.
Label	A (usually) rectangular piece of material, pared leather or paper, applied to the spine which carries the title and sometimes the name of the author. As opposed to the more common prac-

tice of stamping the title and author's name into the binding itself, then inking or gilding the indentations.

Limited edition	Please see special chapter on this subject
Limp binding	Those books whose bindings are not based on boards. Most frequently found in inspirational verse books, Bibles, Torahs, Books of Mormon, etc. Such books have the great and wonderful advantage of lying flat when opened. They often have Yapp edges (q.v.)
Loose	In a catalog, this word indicates that the binding or casing has separated from the signatures. The word "shaken" is also used to indicate such a condition.
Manuscript	Latin: *manu* (hand) and *script* (written). Steinbeck wrote most of his books by hand with a soft leaded pencil on yellow legal pads. When typed, these holograph manuscripts became "typescripts." The manuscript of *The Grapes of Wrath* is in the University of Virginia in Charlottesville. Before the age of printing (c. 1455), all book were manuscripts.
Marbled	The decorative imitation of marble patterns usually of edges and end papers. Some books appear in marbled boards.
Moire'	French: Watered silk. Most commonly refers paste-downs of this pattern. It has a colorful wavy pattern and is quite beautiful. The Franklin Library books have moire' endpapers.
Monograph	A scholarly work, usually an article or pamphlet (but can be book size) on a specific and limited single subject. The articles in academic or professional journals are commonly monographs.
Morocco	One of the best leathers for book-binding. Made from goatskin, it is beautiful and durable. It can be seen in practically any color.

Out-of-print	Abbr. "o.p." A book that is no longer in production and cannot be purchased new. One must resort to the used book market or a remainder house to obtain an o.p. book.
Pagination	The sequential numbering of the pages. The numbers can be Hindu-Arabic (1, 2, 3, etc.) or Roman (i, ii, iii, iv, etc.) and may be placed at the top or bottom of the page. The pagination of a book may be an essential point in determining its edition or issue.
Parchment	A writing surface much like vellum, prepared from the skins of sheeps or goats. The word originates from a blending of a Latin *Pergamina* with *Parthica Pellis* (Parthian skin). Writing material prepared at Pergamum (now Bergama). Some modern paper products are made to resemble parchment. In the past, important legal documents, diplomas, etc., were made of parchment, hence the reference to one's college diploma as a "sheepskin."
Parts	Or part-issue. The publishing of material in serial parts in newspaper or magazine form. These parts mat be assembled and edited and published in book form. All of Dickens' books appeared first in parts except for *Household Worlds* and *Great Expectations*. Charles Lever, Thackeray, and other were first published in parts.
Pirated edition	A book published without the permission of the copyright holder and often without his or her knowledge. Such books are forbidden importation and are illegal. Prior to the international copyright law of 1893, "pirating" was practically routine. American publishers pirated English authors and vice versa. Dickens was furious at American publishers for pirating his works as is evident in *American Notes*.
	Pirating of modern authors is common in the Far East, particularly in Taiwan. Taiwan edi-

tions are so common that one even sees them listed in catalogs.

Presentation

A copy of a book unmistakable in identity as having been presented by the author. A mere autograph is not enough. These are special copies, not just inscribed or signed. Such books often have a special presentation page, usually numbered.

Private press

The terms "private press" and "fine press" are often used interchangeably. A private press is one that is usually owned and operated by one person or a few people. They produce whatever pleases them and may or may not work with a profit motive. If they do exceptionally good work, they may earn the designation "fine press." Typical of fine presses are Kelmscott, Doves, Golden Crockerel, and Ashendene. However, a private press or a small press is not necessarily a fine press.

There are hundreds of private presses in the United States and their work varies from disgraceful to exemplary. Some of their products become collectors' items.

Provenance

The personal history of a book's ownership. Notes, stamps, bookplates, signatures, etc., are evidence constituting provenance. Obviously, the provenance has little or no interest to collectors unless it consists of material associated with well-known persons. Provenance is the evidence by which association copies are identified. For example, Paul Revere engraved a bookplate for Isaiah Thomas, the patriot printer. Thomas's bookplate in a copy of Webster's *Compendious Dictionary* (1807) would be interesting provenance.

Rarity

The book you want and can't find. A borrowed book that has been returned.

Carter devotes nearly three pages to this subject in his *ABC for Book Collectors*, but perhaps Paul

Angle's definition will suffice: "Important, desirable, and hard to get."

Rebacked

Old books often give out at the spine while the boards and text remain sound. When the spine has been replaced, the book is said to be "rebacked." Rebinding replaces boards (or at least the covering), spine and all.

Remaindered

Sometimes a publisher will over-estimate the market for a book. Suppose he produces 10,000 copies in a first printing. Only 6,000 copies sell. In order to recover part of his investment, he sells the remainder to a firm that specializes in marketing such books. A firm of that nature is called a "remainder house." The publisher sells to the remainder house, which can then sell the books for a fraction of the original retail price. Such a book is said to be remaindered.

Review copy

Publishers routinely send copies of new books to newspaper and magazine book reviewers as a part of their publicity program. Such books are usually stamped "review copy" or they have "review copy" slips enclosed or attached. Greedily coveted by collectors. My review copy of *East of Eden* is not for sale.

Shaken

Perhaps a little less loose than "loose" (q.v.).

Signed copy

A book autographed (signed) by the author and only by the author. Any other signature may be interesting but is merely provenance, not a signed copy.

Slip case

A box or case made to contain one or more books. The LEC and Heritage Press books are issued in slip cases, for example. The LEC *Of Mice and Men* is a single volume; the LEC *The Grapes of Wrath* is two volumes. The Washington Square Press *The Divine Comedy* is in three volumes, in slipcases. Limited editions are often "boxed" or in slipcase. In collecting, the slipcase bears the same relationship to the book(s) as a dust jacket does to the book it covers. A "boxed" book without its "box" is incomplete.

Solander case Originally a box made in the form of a book to contain botanical specimens, etc. From D.C. Solander (1736-1782), a protege of Linnaeus. The book-shaped box was so convenient, it was adapted to contain *parts* (q.v.) pamphlets, book-lets, letters, fragile books, etc.

State See special chapter on "First Editions."

Sunned The dye used in leather or cloth bindings will usually fade if exposed to sunlight over a pro-longed period. It is nearly always the spines that will be affected as they are the parts exposed. With white or pale bindings or dust jackets, the spines may be browned or sun-tanned. Sunlight is one of the mortal enemies of books.

Three-decker A work in three volumes most characteristic of 18th and 19th century novels. A. Edward Newton was one of the several noted collectors of three-deckers. It is common for valuable old three-deckers to be contained in custom-made solander cases.

Uncut Referring to the edges of a book, as opposed to "cut." "Untrimmed" is the same as "uncut." An uncut book has rough, uneven edges whereas "cut" or "trimmed" edges are smooth and uni-form. Almost all modern mass-produced books are trimmed.

Unopened Books wherein the leaves have not been cut loose by the printer's knife. A leaf is a sheet of paper in a book which has a page of print on each side. In an unopened book, the leaves are still joined where one would expect the edges to be. An unopened book has obviously not been read.

N.B.: Do not confuse "uncut" and "unopened." Knowing the difference is a shibboleth in the book world.

Vanity press	Printers and binders will manufacture your book if you want to pay for the work. There are firms the specialize in publishing books for which the author pays all of the expenses. Such businesses are known as "vanity presses." One of the best known of these is Vantage Press of New York. It is entirely possible for a book to be quite successful by being self-produced.
Variant	Copies of an edition that exhibit some difference from the accepted standard. Binding variants are the most common. The first edition of *Cannery Row* is buff. There is a canary yellow variant. The first edition of *The Log of the Sea of Cortez* is maroon. There is an aqua green variant. Then there are variants of reprints. The Modern Library reprints abound in variants—bindings, top edge staining, jackets, etc.
Vellum	Fine parchment prepared from calfskin. Old French *velin* from *veel, veal*. Besides being an excellent material on which to write or print, many old books (and a few recent ones) were bound in vellum.
Wrappers	"In wrappers" refers to books originally issued in paper covers. Advance copies, proof copies and review copies are usually issued in wrappers. Few in number and susceptible to deterioration, they are in terrific demand by collectors. A mint first edition of *Cannery Row* is worth less than $100; an advance copy in wrappers is quoted by Van Allen Bradley at "$500. Perhaps more."
Yapp edges	About 1860 a London bookman invented the over-lapping flaps on limp leather bindings. This type of binding is so common with Bibles, prayer books, missals, etc., it is called "divinity circuit."
Yellowbacks	Cheap books published for sale in railway stations in Britain in the 19th century. They are usually yellow in color, hence the common designation. Other colors of such books exist. Fine original copies are scarce and dear.

ABBREVIATIONS

EVERY TRADE, PROFESSION, craft, hobby, or racket has its own jargon, argot, or terminology. In many cases, the vocabulary is in the form of portmanteau words, acronyms, or abbreviations.[45] The book world is no exception. It is difficult to make sense of a bookseller's catalog without some familiarity with the terminology employed, much of which will be in the form of abbreviations. There is a certain lack of uniformity in the abbreviations, some difference in British and American usage, and no list could be absolutely exhaustive, but the following may prove useful:

AB	*AB Bookman's Weekly.*
ABAA	Antiquarian Bookseller's Association of America.
ABPC	American Book Press Current.
A.D.	Autograph document (unsigned).
A.D.s.	Autograph document signed.
Ads.	Advertisements.

---

[45]Portmanteau words are words formed by combining two words, such as "smog" ("smoke" plus "fog") and "brunch" ("breakfast" plus "lunch"). An acronym is made from initial letter(s) of several words. Radio detecting and ranging adds up to RADAR. "Flak" derives from Fleiger Abwehr Kanonen ("anti-aircraft artillery"). "Gestapo" is from Geheime Staats Polezei ("Secret State Police").

Advts.	Advertisements.
A.e.g.	All edges gold (gilt).
A.L.	Autograph letter (unsigned).
A.L.s.	Autograph letter, signed.
A.Ms.s.	Autograph manuscript, signed.
B.A.R.	Book Auction Records (Not Browning Automatic Rifle in the book trade).
B.c.e.	Book club edition.
Bd.	Bound.
Bdg.	Binding.
Bds.	Boards.
BOMC	Book of the Month Club.
BPC	Book Prices Current.
C & P	Collated and Perfect.
Cat.	Catalog.
Cent.	Century.
Cf.	Calf.
Cl.	Cloth.
Col(d)	Color(ed). As in color plates, colored endpapers.
Cont.	Contemporary.
Cont'd	Continued.
CWO	Cash with order. (Not Chief Warrant Officer).
Dec.	Decorated.
D.j.	Dust jacket (American usage).
D.w.	Dust wrapper (British usage)
Ed.	Edition, edited, editor.
Ed. dlx.	Edition deluxe.
E.p.	End paper(s).
Eng(f).	Ex-library.
f.	Fine.
Facs.	Facsimile.
Fcp.	Foolscap (paper).
Fl.	Flourished. Lived during the time period.
Fp.	Frontispiece.
F. widj	Fine with dust jacket.
G.	Good (condition)
Gt.	Gilt.
G.e.	Gilt edge(s).
G.t.	Gilt top.

Hf.	Half, as in hf. mco. (half morocco)
Hf. bd.	Half bound.
ILAB	International League of Antiquarian Booksellers.
I.p.	In print, i.e., available as a new book.
Ill.	Illustrated, illustration(s)
Imp.	Imperial (paper)
Impft.	Imperfect.
Inscr.	Inscribed, inscription.
Imit. lea.	Imitation leather (binding).
Intro.	Introduction
ISBN	International Standard Book Number.
Ital.	Italics.
LC	Library of Congress.
LEC	Limited Editions Club.
Lev.	Levant Morocco (leather).
Lge.	Large, as in lge. 8vo.
Ll.	Leaves.
L.p.	Large paper.
L.s.	Letter (not autograph) signed.
Ltd. ed.	Limited edition.
M.	Mint.
Mor.	Morocco (leather).
M.e.	Marbled edges.
Ms(s).	Manuscript(s).
N.d.	No date (of publication).
N.p.	No place (of publication).
Obl.	Oblong.
OED	Oxford English Dictionary
O.p.	Out of print.
Or., orig.	Original.
Otw.	Otherwise.
p., pp.	Page, pages (Not pg(s). Pg. means pregnant.)
Pict.	Pictorial
Pt(s).	Plate(s)
PMLA.	Publication of the Modern Language Association. (A journal of the MLA).
Pol.	Polished.
Port.	Portrait.
P.p.	Privately published.

Prelim.	Preliminary leaves.
Pres.	Presentation (copy).
Pseud.	Pseudonym(ous) (ly).
Pt(s).	Part(s).
Ptd.	Printed.
Pub.	Published, publisher.
PW.	*Publisher's Weekly.*
R.e.	Red edges.
Rev.	Revised, revision.
SASE	Self addressed stamped envelope.
Sgd.	Signed.
Sig.	Signature.
Sm.	Small. As in "sm. 12mo."
Sq.	Square. As in "sq. 4to."
Swd.	Sewed.
T.e.g.	Top edge gilt.
Thk.	Thick. As in "thk. 8vo."
T.l.s.	Typed letter signed.
T.p.	Title page.
Ts.	Typescript.
Ung., unbd.	Unbound.
V.d.	Various dates (No. Not venereal disease).
V.g.	Very good.
Vol(s).	Volume(s).
W.	Worn. As in "v.g. in w. d.j."
W.a.f.	With all faults
Wps.	Wrappers
Y.e.	Yellow edges
Yp.e.	Yapp edges

For an exhaustive and encyclopedic work on abbreviations, consult *World Guide to Abbreviations,* edited by Paul Spillner (New York: R.R. Bowker., 2nd ed.), 1295 pp. in 3 vols. This reference lists 50,000 internationally accepted Roman alphabet abbreviations used by government, commercial, cultural, religious and other elements of society and civilization in 120 countries.

For common Latin abbreviations and phrases apt to be encountered in bibliographic and literary works, see the following section.

LATIN PHRASES, WORDS, AND ABBREVIATIONS

COMMONLY FOUND IN ENGLISH

LANGUAGE PUBLICATIONS

THE VOCABULARY OF the English language is about 60 percent Latin derivatives (approximately half of which have come to us through French). For more than 1500 years, Latin was the language of the ubiquitous Church and of most of the scholarship in Europe. There was always some Greek writing being done and a minute but important amount of work in Hebrew. For several centuries, excellent writing, especially in mathematics and physical science, was done in Granada in Arabic. We inherited, however, very few Hebrew words (sabbath, jubilee, canon, behemoth, etc.) and only a few dozen Arabic words found a permanent place in the English vocabulary. Such words as azimuth, zenith, nadir, horizon, and algebra show our indebtedness to the Arabs for their navigational skills and their mathematical ingenuity. Words like elixir, syrup, alkali, alcohol, and (al) chem (y) istry reveal their influence upon our medieval science.

However, all of the contributions of Arabic, Hebrew, Persian, and all other languages (except Greek) make up only about 5 percent of the English vocabulary. Greek constitutes a critically important 10 percent. Paradoxically, English is only 25 percent English, i.e., vocabulary derived from Anglo-Saxon (and its sister language, Old Norse). English grammar and structure is Germanic, but its vocabulary is overwhelmingly Latin. And since hundreds of Latin words, phrases and abbreviations still exist in English—particularly in bibliographic and bibliophilic English—it behooves the book lover to be familiar with them.

The following makes no claim to be even an abridged dictionary of Latin terms, but is intended as a review of key prepositions, conjunctions, abbreviations and common phrases often seen in reading and research. It is virtually axiomatic that the older the book, the more frequent is the Latin influence. The trend in modern English is to minimize the use of Latin, that is, using plain English terms where Latin would have been appropriate in former generations. Still, the vast majority of the standard Latin literary terms seem to be here to stay.

Abbreviation	Latin Word or Phrase	English Translation
	ab	Prefix. Away, away from; as in "abduct."
	ad	Prefix. To, toward, for; as in "advance," "adhere."
	ad hoc	For this (only occasion).
	ad hominem	Toward the man. Said of an argument. Attacking the man instead of his argument.
	ad infinitum	To infinity. Unending.
ad lib.	ad libitum	At liberty. At will.
	ad nauseum	Lit., to illness. To boredom.
	ad valorem	According to the value (taxes).
	alias	Otherwise (known as).
	alibi	Elsewhere.
A.D.	Anno Domini	(The) Year (of) (our) Lord. Not "After Death." Dates from the *birth* of Jesus, not some 33 years later.

a.p.	*Anni praesentis*	In the present year.
	ante	Before.
	ante bellum	Before the war. In the U.S., the Civil War.
A.M.	*Ante Meridian*	Before noon.
	apud	By, at, with. *Apud me, "at my place." Apud Deo,* "with God."
	caveat emptor	Let the buyer beware.
c.,ca.	*circa*	Around. Used only with dates, as in "c. 1500 B.C."
	circum	Around. As in Circumlocution Office.
cf.	*confer*	Compare.
	contra	Against. "Pros & cons" should be "Pros & contras."
	corpus	Body. *Corpus delicti* is New Latin for "body of the crime." *Corpus juris,* "body of the law." *Corpus Christi,* "Body of Christ."
c	*c*	With, *c* aquae, "with water."
	cum	With honor. Magna cum laude,
	cum laude	"With great honor." Summa cum laude, "With highest honor."
	de	Preposition and prefix meaning "from" or "away" as in "deduct."
	de facto	From the facts, In fact.
	de jure	From the law. In law.
e.g.	*exempli gratia*	Example given. For example.
	ergo	Therefore.
	et.	And.
et al.	*et alii*	And others.
etc.	*et cetera*	And so on.
et seq.	*et sequens*	And following.
et us.	*et uxor*	And spouse.
	e(x), ex	Out. Out of. As in *E(x) Pluribus Unum,* "Out of the many, one."
	ex cathedra	From the chair, i.e., official, authorative. A *cathedral* is the location of the bishop's chair.
e.o., ex. off.	*ex officio*	From the office, i.e., by virtue of office or position.

	ex post facto	A law or rule made after the commission of an act forbidden by that law or rule.
Ibid.	*Ibidem*	In the same place (book). Indicates "ditto the above reference" in a footnote.
i.e.	*id est*	That is.
i.q.	*idem quod*	The same as.
	in re	In the matter of (Not "in reference.").
I.N.R.I.	*Iesus Nazarenus Rex Iudaeorum*	Jesus of Nazareth King of the Jews
	in situ	In place.
	in vivo	In life.
	infra	Below. *Vide infra,* "see below," as in a book.
	ipse dixit	"Himself says." An unsupported statement.
	ipso facto	By the fact itself.
	inter	Between, among.
	inter alia	Among others.
loc. cit.	*Loco citato*	Place cited. Used in footnotes.
	magnum opus	Great work, masterpiece.
	mea culpa	My fault.
	modus operandi	Method of operation.
	modus vivendi	Mode of living.
	ne plus ultra	Nothing more beyond. Nothing better. The best.
	nihil	Nothing.
	nulli secundus	Second to none.
	non compos mentis	Not mentally competent.
	non sequitur	It does not follow. Said of a false conclusion in argumentation and logic.
N.B.	*nota bene*	Note well.
	nunc	Now. *Quid nunc?* "What now?"
	obiter dictum	A statement in passing, an incidental remark.
	opus	Work, i.e., a creative work of art. Used to catalogue music, as "opus 7."
op. cit.	*opere citato*	Work cited. As in footnotes.

	passim	Here and there or throughout. As "p. 23, p. 41, et passim."
	per annum	Each year. By the year.
	per aspera	Through ambition.
per cent.	*per centem*	Through a hundred. Of a hundred.
	per diem	By the day.
	per se	As such.
	post	After. Antonym of *ante*.
	post hoc ergo	*After this therefore because of this.* One of the classical logical fallacies in argumentation.
P.M.	*post meridian*	After noon.
p.m.	*post mortem*	After death.
P.S.	*post scriptum*	After writing.
P.P.S.	*post postscriptum*	After the postscript.
	prima facie	At first appearance.
	pro	Before. In front of. As in *pro fane*, "before the temple."
	pro	For. In support of.
	pro bono publico	For the public good.
	propter	Because.
s.l.	*sine loco*	Without place. No place of publication shown.
s.n.	*sine nomine*	Without name. No name of publisher indicated.
	sine qua non	Without which nothing. Absolutely essential.
S.P.Q.R.	*Senatu Populusque Romanus*	The Senate & People of Rome.
	status quo	The state of things as they are.
	sub	Under. Below. As in *sub mensa,* "under the table."
	sub rosa	Lit., "under the rose." Secret, private. From the Roman custom of hanging a rose over the lintel of a private meeting room.
s.v.	*sub verbo (or voce)*	Under the word or heading.
sup.	*supra*	Above. *Vide supra,* "see above."
	terra	Earth. *Terra Firma,* "solid ground." *Terra incognita,* "unknown territory."

	ultra	Beyond. Ultra violet—beyond the violet band in the spectrum. *Ulterior* is a derivative.
v.	*verso*	Left-hand page in a book. The "flip" side of the *recto,* which is the right-hand side of a page.
	vademecum	Lit. "take with me," some thing one carries every where. A book of verses might be a *vademecum* for Omar Khayyam.
	verbatim	Word for word. From Latin *verbym,* "word." *In principio erat verbum.* "In the beginning was a word."
	vide	See. *Vide supra, vide infra.*
viz.	*videlicet*	Namely. The author of *Waverly, viz.,* Sir Walter Scott...
	vincit	Conquers, overcomes. Many popular mottoes and aphorisms employ the word: *Vincit omnia veritas, "Truth conquers all." Vincere aut mori,* "To conquer or to die." And many others.
	virtus	Manly excellence. *Virtute, non viris,* "By virtue, not by men."
	vita	Life. *Vita brevis, ars longa.* "Life is brief; art long." *Aqua vitae,* "Water of life."
	vox	Voice. *Vox populi,* "Voice of the people." *Vox Dei.* "Voice of God."
	Vox audita perit, Litera scripta	The voice that is heard, perishes; the letter that is written, abides.

THE SYSTEM OF ROMAN NUMERALS

IF YOU HAVE trouble figuring out which pope John XXIII was or which king Louis XVI was, you might profit from a review of the numbering system we inherited from ancient Rome. Besides popes and kings, the Roman numerals are often used for paginating, or by publishers for indicating the dates of publications. Besides these functions, the numerals are commonly found on monuments and inscriptions.

Books will sometimes have the publishing date on the title page in Roman numerals and the copyright date on the verso in English (actually Arabic or Hindu) numerals. If you have difficulty deciphering the publication date, you may miss vital information for a book collector. If the title page reads MDCCCVII and the copyright pages shows 1802, it is likely that you have a first edition?

The following is a concise review of this ancient but still viable system.

I equals 1   IV equals 4 (i.e., "I" on the left
II equals 2   side is subtracted from "V").
III equals 3   V equals 5

VI equals 6	CC is 200
VII equals 7	CCC is 300
VIII equals 8	CD is 400 ("C" subtracted from
IX equals 9 ("I" subtracted from "X")	"D", 500).
X equals 10	D is 500
XI equals 11, XII is 12, and so on.	DC is 600
XV is 15	DCC is 700
XX is 20	DCCC is 800
XXX is 30	CM is 900 ("C", 100, subtracted
XL is 40 ("X" on the left or	from "M", 1000).
subtracted from "L")	M is 1000
L is 50	MM is 2000
LX is 60 and so on.	MCM is 1900 Ergo, MCMLXXIX
XC is 90 ("X" subtracted from "C")	is 1979. MCMLXXX is 1980
C is 100	

The decimal (decem, "ten") system is based upon the human hand. Remember that the "I" is a symbol for one finger. The "V" for the bifurcation made by the thumb and the remaining four digits. The "X" is two "V's". "C" stands for Latin centem, 100 and "M" for Latin mille, 1000. "D" is half (demi) of 1000. Then it is just a simple matter of adding and subtracting letters.

The collector should practice with the Roman system until he is adept in deciphering it rapidly. Suppose you are in a book store looking at an old book. The publishing date is MDCCXLII and the author is Joseph Addison. Addison died in MDCCXIX. Could this be a first edition?

The difference between the right date and almost the right date is like the difference between the lightning and the lightning bug. (Apologies to Mark Twain).

BOOKS ABOUT BOOKS

IN EVERY CRAFT or hobby there are books on the subject. You can find books about thimbles, dolls, paperweights, book-ends, early automobiles, letter openers, farm implements, and what not. It should come as no surprise that there is an extensive accumulation of books about book collecting, printing, binding, publishing, illustrations, paper, and every conceivable element and feature of the world of books.

In an ordinary book, the bibliography is a simple thing. The author lists his own sources and perhaps some books for further reading on a subject. However, in the world of book collecting, the word "bibliography" assumes a meaning of its own. It denotes a comprehensive listing (with descriptions, dates and places of publication, points, variant, reprint, translations, etc.) of the publications of a certain author. Bibliographies are also compiled on specific subjects, e.g., a bibliography of electronics.

There is a bibliography of nearly every established author. Sometimes more than one.[46] There are even many bibliographies

---

[46]For example, there are the Hayashi bibliography and the Goldstone & Payne bibliography of Steinbeck.

of obscure, mediocre, or forgotten writers. There are bibliographies of bibliographies.

If your book buying has led you into collecting a certain author, check with a librarian or book dealer about a bibliography of that author. A bibliography is to a collector as a road map is to a traveler.

If you are collecting one or more contemporary authors, as I would suggest, it is probable that no bibliography exists. In this case, you may write to the author or to the publisher concerning the publications in which you are interested.

Many books will list the books already published by the author of the book you happen to be examining ... usually on the verso of the half-title. If you were collecting Peter Benchley, you could turn to that page in a copy of *The Deep* and find "Books by Peter Benchley": *The Deep, Jaws, Time and a Ticket.* Sometimes, such lists are found on the dust jacket. It is helpful information but often tricky. Publishers may list only the books of that author that they have published. If the author has been published by more than one firm, those titles may not be listed.

Consult *Books in Print* (New York: R.R. Bowker Co.).[47] Your local city or county library should have current copies. There you can find the titles your author has produced since he or she has been published.

Besides author bibliographies, there are bibliographies covering various subjects and genres. The dime novel is charted. Detective fiction, science fiction, Western fiction, erotica, medical books, railroading, math, science, art, etc.; all have their reference bibliographies. The best reference for nonfiction subjects is *Subject Guide to Books in Print*. About 400,000 titles are listed.

If, as Carlyle wrote, "The true university is a collection of books," then we need to have a catalog of the "university." The following list of books about books should give you a fair hint of the vast amount of reading available on the fascinating subject of books, *per se.*

---

[47]R.R. Bowker Co., 1180 Avenue of the Americas, New York, N.Y., 10056, is justifiably called the publisher's publisher. For the greatest selection of books about books, write for their catalog.

AN ANNOTATED BIBLIOGRAPHY OF BOOK ABOUT BOOKS

Ahearn, Allen and Patricia, *Book Collecting* (NY: Putnam, 1995). A veritable encyclopedia of data, lists, etc. with emphasis on the first books of collectible authors. Superb work.

Ahearn, Allen and Patricia, *A Collection of First Books* (Bethesda, Md.: Quill & Brush Books, 1984). Lists 1,035 first editions of authors' first books and their market prices.

Ahearn, Allen and Patricia, *Collected Books, the Guide to Values* (NY: Putnam, 1991). Virtually the only authoritative price guide available. Meticulous research and presentation.

Anderson, Charles B., et al., editors, *A Manual on Bookselling* (New York: ABA, dist. by R.R. Bowker Co., 1969), 271 pp., incl. index. 34 chapters by authorities on each phase, plus extensive appendix for professional booksellers.

Bennett, Paul A., editor, *Books and Printing, A Treasury for Typophiles* (Cleveland: World Pub. Co., Rev. ed., 1963). 430 pp. incl. index. An anthology of articles by excellent authorities.

Bradley, Van Allen, *The Book Collector's Handbook of Values* (New York: G.P. Putnam's Sons, 3rd ed., rev & enlarged) 1978-79 edition, 590 pp. An encyclopedia of rare books for collectors, dealers and librarians. This reference gives the prices that books have actually sold for in real transactions. If you could have only one book about books, this would be it.

Blank, Jacob, editor, *Bibliography of American Literature* (New Haven: Yale Univ. Press, Vol. I, 1955). The definitive reference on American literature. This work sold for $25 per vol. in 1955. Prohibitive for the average bookworm but may be used in a library.

Boutell, Henry S., *First Editions of Today and How to Tell Them* (Berkeley: Peacock Press, 1964) 4th ed. rev. by Wanda Underhill. A classic, highly desirable and useful but difficult to acquire as it is a favorite with professional book people.

Bowers, Fredson, *Principles of Bibliographical Description* (Newark: Oak Knoll, 1995). Softcover. 536 pp. Dr. Bowers' reputation at the University of Virginia and as a bibliographer is absolutely unrivaled. This is the ultimate authority.

Carter, John, *ABC for Book Collectors*, 7th Ed. (Newark: Oak Knoll, 1995). Revised by Nicolas Barker and entirely reset; incorporates much new material and amendments since the previous edition.

Chappell, Warren, *A Short History of the Printed Word* (New York: Alfred A. Knopf, 1970). A beautiful book, designed by Chappell, superbly illustrated, well written, it is an excellent history of the production of books.

Cockerell, Douglas, *Bookbinding, and the Care of Books* (Lyons and Burford). Softcover. 320 pp. A comprehensive exposition of the bookbinder's art.

Field, Eugene, *The Love Affair of a Bibliomaniac* (New York: Scribners', 1896). Rambling reminiscences in book collecting by a poet and veteran collector of fine taste. A pleasure to read.

Greenfield, Jane, *The Care of Fine Books* (Lyons and Burford). Softcover. 224 pp. Cleaning and repair, storage and handling. Illustrated professional advice.

Haller, Margaret, *The Book Collector's Fact Book* (New York: Arco Pub. Co., 1976). A practical introduction to rare and valuable books, including the "new antiques," i.e., books on photography, movies, comics, as well as modern first editions. Arranged as a glossary (like Carter's *ABC*), this reference work is a useful addition to your library.

Hanff, Helene, *84 Charing Cross Road* (New York: Grossman Pub. Div. of Viking Press, deluxe ed., 1975). The book lover cannot find 97 pages of more delightful reading than this. It is an exchange of letters between the author and a London book shop at the address in the title. It is beautifully done and provides a good insight into the characteristics of humanity and decency of most bookmen.

Harrison, Frederick, *A Book About Books* (London: John Murry, 1943). A good example of the sophisticated book for the advanced bibliophile with a fine historical background.

Hodson, Anthony, *Great Libraries* (New York: G.P. Putnam's Sons, 1970). 320 pp., index. This large "coffee table" book includes glossary, maps, 60 illustrations in color and 330 black & white pictures. It discusses 32 of the world's greatest libraries. The textual material is brief but informative.

Horton, Carolyn, *Cleaning and Preserving Bindings and Related Materials* (Chicago: Library Technology Program, American Library Assn., 2nd ed., rev., 1969). This 87-page publication is one of a series in

"Conservation of Library Materials." Horton's book, with the John Carter *ABC* (see entry above) should be essential reading for collectors.

Hutton, Laurence, *From the Books of* (New York: Harper & Row, 1892). Erudite commentary about his own library by a scholar whose *Literary Landmarks of London* (1885) and *Talks in a Library* (1905) are also worth reading.

Iacone, Salvatore J., *The Pleasures of Book Collecting* (New York: Harper & Row, 1976). 303 pp. including index, bibliography, and a list of members of ABAA. Presented in three parts, this book has many useful features including excellent, relevant photographic illustrations.

Johnson, Merle, *American First Editions* (Waltham: Mark Press, rev. & enlarged by Jacob Blank, 4th ed., 1969). A standard reference which, like Boutell, is very difficult to find. This is one of the most convenient books for dealers and collectors; hence owners are reluctant to part with their copies.

McMurtrie, Douglas C., *The Book, the Story of Printing and Book Making Illustrated* (London: Oxford, 1943). (11th ptg. 1976). 676 pp., including index & bibliography. From cave paintings, cuneiform, hieroglyphics, through Greek and Roman writing, with a history and evolution of the alphabet to modern printing.

Madigan, Thomas F., *Word Shadows of the Great* (New York: Stokes Co., 1930). A meticulous work of learning on the lure and lore of autograph collecting, including those in books, manuscripts, and letters.

Magee, David, *Infinite Riches* (New York: Eriksson, 1973). Memoirs of a distinguished Anglo-American bookman. A delight and an education for the book lover.

Mott, Frank Luther, *Golden Multitudes* (New York: Macmillan, 1947) 357 pp., including index and lists of best sellers from earliest Colonial days. A scholarly yet easy-to-read history of the best seller phenomenon. A rich anecdotal history as well as wealth of professional and statistical data. As delightful as a novel.

Muir, Percy H., *Book Collecting as a Hobby* (New York: Knopf, 1947). Muir is the author of the authoritative *Points*, 2-vol. work of erudition published in 1931. *Book Collecting as a Hobby* is one of the best for the serious amateur.

Newton, A. Edward, *The Amenities of Book Collecting and Kindred Affections* (Boston: Atlantic Monthly Press, 1918). Prof. Liebert of Yale once remarked that this book of Newton's had probably converted more people to book collecting than any other, which is no exaggeration. I have also read and recommend *End Papers* (1933), *A Magnificent Farce and other Diversions of a Book Collector* (1921), and *This Book Collecting Game*. He wrote many others. In fact, Newton was so prolific that his works are themselves the subject of intense collecting.

Pearson, Edmund, *Books in Black and Red* (New York: Macmillan, 1924). Lavishly illustrated and delightful book for the collector who cannot afford museum pieces. Pearson also did a bibliography on dime novels.

Pearson, Edmund, *Queer Books* (New York: Doubleday, Doran, 1928). Informative and interesting narrative about temperance novels, propaganda novels, gift books, annual and other strange and unorthodox publications.

Petersen, Clarence, *The Bantam Story, Thirty Years of Paperback Publishing* (New York: Bantam Books). 2nd ed. rev. 1975. 136 pp. plus appendix listing Bantam paperbacks in print. Particularly appropriate for collectors of first paperback editions.

Quale, Eric, *The Collector's Book of Books* (New York: Clarkson N. Potter, 1971). Beautifully illustrated in color, this might be called the picture book of book collecting. Competent text.

Quale, Eric, *The Collector's Book of Children's Books* (New York: Clarkson N. Potter, 1971). In this book, Quale does for children's books what he did for books in general. It is especially helpful because it permits the collector to see what the collectable books look like—an advantage not to be slighted.

Randall, David, *Dukedom Large Enough* (New York: Random House, 1973). Memoirs of one of the great bookmen of the 20th century. If you were conducting a course in book appreciation and the book trade, you might assign the late Mr. Randall's *Dukedom* as a text.

Rees-Moog, William, *How to Buy Rare Books* (Oxford: Phaidon-Christie's, 1985). 2nd impression 1988. A practical guide to the antiquarian book market. This is Christie's collectors guide.

Rodger, William, *Official Guide to Old Books and Autographs* (Florence, Ala: House of Collectibles, 1976). 444 pp., including ads for the House of Collectibles, a $5.95 paperback of poor physical quality. My copy has several permanently creased pages. Many typo errors. How did this get to be the "official" guide? From what authority? Many prices shown are not representative of the market. Caveat emptor.

Rosenbach, Abraham Solomon Wolf, *Books and Bidders, the Adventures of a Bibliophile* (Boston: Little, Brown & Co. 1927). The big league of book collecting. Dr. Rosenbach was a book finder for Morgan, Huntington and other great collectors for many years. Spellbinding for the book lover. Illustrated with photographs. Rosenbach is the author of several other books on our subject, e.g., *A Book Hunter's Holiday* (NY: Houghton-Mifflin, 1936). Rosenbach was a legend in his own time and still spoken of as a sage and a patriarch.

Rostenberg, Leona, and Madeleine B. Stern, *Old and Rare* (New York: Abner Schram, 1974). 210 pp. of carefully written memorabilia of years of scholarly experience, much of it in Europe. For the more advanced collector.

Starrett, Vincent, *Born in a Bookshop* (Norman: University of Ilahoma Press, 1965). One of the many books about books and authors by Starrett, whose publications began as long ago as 1918. Subtitled "Chapters from the Chicago Renascence," and like all of Starrett's books, it is informative and accurate. Illustrated with great old photographs of bookmen and authors. 325 pp., indexed.

Steele, Colin, complier, *Major Libraries of the World, A Selective Guide* (New York: Bowker, 1976), 479 pp. In order to see the great book collections of the world, one needs to know where to go. This is the finest book available on that subject.

Stewart, Seumas, *Book Collecting* (New York: Dutton, 1973). A modern guide for the serious collector. Crowded with useful information and interesting commentary. Especially suitable for the scholar of literature.

Tannen, Jack, *How to Identify and Collect American First Editions* (New York: Arco Pub. Co. 1976). 147 pp. incl. index. Lists more than 270 publishers and their methods of denoting first editions. The author has been a dealer in books for 50 years and offers useful advice and suggestions in addition to identifying first editions.

Thomas, Alan G., *Fine Books* (New York: G.P. Putnam's Sons, 1967). Printed in Germany, this 120 pp. square-format book is of beautiful quality. It is worth cherishing for the illustrations alone. Designed for the sophisticated and discriminating bibliophile.

Thompson, James Westfall, *Byways in Bookland* (Berkeley: University of California Book Arts Club, 1935). A series of ten brilliant essays bound in a limited and numbered edition.

Webber, Winslow L., *Books About Books* (Boston: Hale, Cusman & Flint, 1937). A bibliography of books about books and book collecting. In order to appreciate the enormous number of such books and their variety, the collector should at least scan this impressive work. It is a good source when a particularly elusive old bibliography is sought.

West, Herbert F., *Modern Book Collecting for the Impecunious Amateur* (Boston: Little, Brown & Co., 1936). A notable effort and a useful book, but Mr. West, like most writers on the subject, tends to backslide into writing for the affluent and sophisticated. He is also the author of *The Mind on the Wing* and other books.

Wheatly, H.B., *The Dedication of Books* (London: Elliot Stock, 1887). A chapter in literary history. A little esoteric for the beginner but so well done and enlightening in this area that any student bibliophile would enjoy it.

Wilson, Robert A., *Modern Book Collecting* (Newark: Oak Knoll). Softcover. 276 pp. One of the most useful books of its kind available today.

Winterich, John T., *Collector's Choice* (New York: Greenberg, 1928). Commentary of a first-rate bookman. Winterich is the author of the popular *A Primer of Book Collecting*.

_____ *About Books, A Gathering of Essays* (Berkeley: The Book Arts Club of California, 1941). No particular author is indicated. James D. Hart wrote the introduction to this publication of four of the most famous of bibliophilic essays. The book was issued in 450 numbered copies. Contains the famous essay "Librarians as Enemies of Books."

PERIODICALS

IN ADDITION TO books about books, the collector should be familiar with some of the periodicals that will be helpful to him or her. The most popular and useful of all is *AB Bookman's Weekly*. Book collectors of all descriptions from all over the country place ads in this weekly magazine, and if you wish to buy or sell books, this is the place to look. If one were teaching a course in book collecting, the *AB* would be assigned reading.

In addition to being the "want ad" section of the book world, the *AB Bookman's Weekly* contains timely articles. You can learn of new businesses, sales, conferences, book fairs, etc. It also includes articles on significant collectors and collections, past and present, obituaries, notices, announcements, etc., all of interest to the bibliophile.

If you subscribe, as you should if serious about book collecting, order your AB to be sent FIRST CLASS MAIL (at substantial extra cost) because at the regular periodical rate, it will arrive late.

To subscribe, address:

> *AB Bookman's Weekly*
> P.O. Box AB
> Newark, N.J. 07015

Other periodicals worth looking into include:
>
> *Biblio*
> P.O. Box 10603
> Eugene, OR 97440
>
> *Firsts*
> P.O. Box 65166
> Tucson, AZ 85728

The Sunday magazine sections of the great newspapers usually have book sections which indicate the current national and regional best sellers. They have book reviews and advertisements of the publishers. It is worth while to consult them. The *New York Times Book Review* is particularly well done and worth while.

INDEX

AB Bookman's Weekly, 102, 109, 189, 208-209

Ahearn, 14, 18, 21, 54, 104, 109, 123, 125, 134, 203

alias, 132, 194

Anonyma and Pseudonyma, 134

association copies, 62, 176, 185

association copy, 176

The Author Looks at Format, 64

autograph, 53-55, 185, 189-191, 207

Barnes & Noble, 121

best sellers, 4, 29-30, 32-33, 46, 51, 60, 82-83, 205, 209

Bible, 4, 45-46, 70, 131

binding, 3, 18-19, 26, 47, 49-50, 66, 74, 76, 78, 88, 95, 157, 176, 178, 183, 186-187, 190-191, 201

Blue Ribbon Books, 92, 177

Book Club Edition (BCE), 14, 43, 49-50, 190

The Book of Firsts, 64

bookcase, 79

bookend, 79

bookplate, 61-62, 71-74, 77, 176, 185

bookseller, 60, 66, 76, 98, 100, 103-107, 120, 135, 189

Bowker Annual, 32

Cassell, Ltd., 93

catalog, 162

charity store, 110, 122

Collected Books, the Guide to Values, 14, 109, 125, 134, 203

condition, 6, 11, 13-14, 22-23, 59-76, 86, 88, 100-101, 110, 114, 119-120, 140, 152, 176, 181, 190

dealer, 21-22, 42, 61, 66, 70-71, 88-89, 97-111, 120, 122-123, 126, 150, 160, 202, 207

Dodd Mead & Co., 93

Doubleday, 50, 93, 118, 151, 206

dust jacket/dust wrapper, 11, 47, 49-50, 52, 60-61, 63-69, 83, 88, 99, 102, 107, 118, 121, 124, 150-152, 157, 179, 187, 190, 202

Easton Press, 28, 95, 121

Encyclopedia Britannica, 15, 121, 125

Everyman, 26, 92

ex-lib, 88

fine press, 25, 61, 94-95, 179, 185

first edition, 4-6, 8, 11-19, 22, 26, 49-52, 54, 60, 62, 64, 66, 72, 84, 93, 101-102, 114, 118, 122-124, 150-152, 161, 165, 179-180, 188, 199-200

first impression, 16-17

first printing, 2, 6, 13-14, 17-19, 43, 54-55, 64, 99, 115, 150-151, 179, 186

first state, 17-19, 60, 64, 122, 150, 152

flea market, 109, 119-120, 155

Folio Society, 52, 92

folio, 52, 92, 167-169, 180

foreign language collection, 45

format, 3, 17, 64, 159, 161, 167-169

Franklin Library, 28, 95, 183

Friends of the Library, 55, 73-74, 125-126

Funk and Wagnalls, 92-93

garage sale, 50, 114

Golden Multitudes, 33, 205

Goldstone, Adrian, 54

Grosset & Dunlap, 64, 91, 102

Hawthorne, 43, 93

Henry Holt, 92

Heritage Press, 92, 102, 186

History Book Club, 50-51

incunabula, 21, 29, 111, 182

inscription, 53-55, 73, 191

Internet, 157-166

John Day, 93

Knopf, 93, 178-179, 204-205

library sale, 74

library, 2-5, 9, 15, 28, 46, 50, 55-56, 59, 62-64, 66-67, 71-74, 76-77, 79, 83, 85-90, 92, 95, 98, 102, 110-113, 115, 117, 119, 122-126, 135, 140, 143, 145, 150, 158, 172, 176, 182-183, 188, 191, 202-205

limited edition, 25-26, 28, 183, 191

Limited Editions Club (LEC), 6, 13-14, 26-27, 95, 186, 191

Lippincott, 16, 93

Macmillan, 33, 92, 94, 151, 205-206

manuscript, 15, 91, 179, 183, 190-191

mint, 52, 59, 61-63, 67, 188, 191

Modern Library Books, 64, 92

newsgroup, 161

nickname, 131, 133

Nobel, 15, 35-36, 88, 134

octavo, 77, 167-169

paperback, 7, 63, 68, 76, 102, 118-119, 149-150, 152, 206

Parrish Condition, 59

pen name, 136

pirated, 19, 47, 184

pseudonym, 133, 136, 138, 148, 192

Pulitzer Prize, 6, 13-14, 31, 33, 38-42, 51, 82, 106, 142, 153

Quigley, Michael, 60, 147

Random House, 93, 118, 149, 206

Reprint Society of London, 52

reprint, 13-14, 22, 43, 52, 54, 67, 72, 92, 102, 119, 201

small press, 94, 185

Sun Dial Press, 64, 92

supply and demand, 12, 54

Taugher, Dennis, 157, 161-162, 166

thrift store, 2, 121-122, 124-125

trade edition, 14, 26-27, 60
Triangle Books, 64, 92, 102, 177
University of Indiana Press, 92
vanity press, 93-94, 188
variant, 18-19, 64, 188, 201
very fine, 4, 60-61, 63, 66, 94, 102
very good, 44, 61, 142, 152, 192
Viking Press, 14, 92-93, 178, 204
w.a.f., 99, 192
want list, 102, 115
World Almanac, 39
World Wide Web, 159, 163-166